AC
DIS

D0446064

THE SINGLE GIRL'S GUIDE TO

Meeting
European Men

KATHERINE CHLOÉ CAHOON

GREENLEAF
BOOK GROUP PRESS

Published by Greenleaf Book Group Press
Austin, Texas
www.gbgpress.com

Distributed by Greenleaf Book Group LLC

For ordering information or special discounts for bulk purchases, please contact Greenleaf Book Group LLC at PO Box 91869, Austin, TX, 78709, 512.891.6100.

Design and composition by Greenleaf Book Group LLC
Cover design by Greenleaf Book Group LLC
Black and white illustrations by Andrea Jensen
Cover colorist: Al Doggett

Publisher's Cataloging-In-Publication Data
(Prepared by The Donohue Group, Inc.)
Cahoon, Katherine Chloe.
    The single girl's guide to meeting European men / Katherine Chloe Cahoon.—1st ed.
    p. : ill. ; cm.
    Includes index.
    ISBN: 978-1-60832-058-5
    1. Dating (Social customs)—Europe. 2. Single women—Sexual behavior. 3. Mate selection. 4. Single women—Travel—Europe. I. Title. II. Title: Meeting European men.
HQ800.2 .C342 2010
646.77   2010927215

Part of the Tree Neutral™ program, which offsets the number of trees consumed in the production and printing of this book by taking proactive steps, such as planting trees in direct proportion to the number of trees used: www.treeneutral.com

TreeNeutral

Printed in the United States of America on acid-free paper

10 11 12 13 14 15   10 9 8 7 6 5 4 3 2 1

First Edition

*This book is dedicated to my favorite European men:
Enrique, Joaquín, Olivier, the Spaniards of Kapital
who made my European Scarlett O'Hara fantasy a reality,
and Romantic Danish Party Thrower.*

Contents

Fulfilling Your Personal European Man Fantasy

Every girl leaving for Europe has a different man fantasy. I wanted to be wined and dined by the natives and really get to know their cultures. I wanted to enter a club and be treated like Scarlett O'Hara, with myriads of men bringing me drinks in unison, treating me like a European princess, and arguing over which of them would dance with me. Dare to dream! Well, this fantasy became a reality, and when I had to leave Europe those romantic encounters followed me home. An enormous bouquet of roses arrived at my door on February 14. The enclosure card read, "Happy Day of Valentine from Across the Sea!" and was signed by one of my favorite European men. It came minutes before my American boyfriend was slated to pick me up for a special date. How in the world would I ever explain this one?

My girlfriend's European man fantasy was to create her own erotic memoirs. Her goal was to have a one-night stand with a native in every European country she visited and get laid in unique cultural landmarks. Her fantasy also became a reality. Who says she didn't study her history classes while she was abroad? She even brought them to life! Her liaisons took place at historic sites ranging from the top of the Eiffel Tower to Trafalgar Square. She had decided up front that she didn't want to date these guys long term. Spending time getting to know them would take time away from adding stars to her European Hookup Map. Her motto? "I don't do European boyfriends, and I always hand out Guilt-Free Trip Cards!" She left Europe with a star map suitable for framing.

Another girlfriend had the opposite goal. She wanted to fall in love with a European man. She went to France for an entire year to study and immediately started searching for "the one." She exclusively dated a Frenchman during her first three months, hoping to fall in love with him. Although the two of them really enjoyed each other, she couldn't bring herself to tell him those three important words. During the next few months, she steadily dated another Frenchman. This was followed by two European drive-by boyfriends. Unfortunately, none of them were Mr. European Love of Her Life.

At the midpoint in her stay, my friend doubted that her fantasy would ever come true. Then she went on a love-provoking weekend to Sweden and ran into the man of her dreams. When I say "ran into," I mean that literally. It was like an experience straight out of an old romantic movie where a guy and girl knock into each other, lock eyes, and can't look away. For the next two days they were inseparable—dining together, going out on the town, and dancing the night away. She cried when she had to return to France because the man of her dreams lived in another European country. Was she maybe being a little dramatic? I don't think so. They talked every night over the phone and he used his vacation to visit her the next month. He was an artist and painted a gorgeous portrait of her to express his love. When her year in France was over, she spent a "glorious" month with him in his hometown. Now she is back in America and can't bring herself to fall for any other guy. She stays in close contact with Mr. European Love of Her Life and they are actively planning to live together forever.

THE BOTTOM LINE

So whatever European male fantasy you have, *The Single Girl's Guide to Meeting European Men* will help you turn it into a reality. It will show you how to open the door to meeting these fascinating men. What you do after you walk through that door is up to you.

Road Map to Your Guy-Getting Guide

This book is for single girls wanting to meet desirable European men who are into them and pass by those who are not—without regret. It arose out of several semesters that my girlfriends and I spent studying in Europe. I toured more museums and was tested on more scholarly material than I can ever remember, but one of the most meaningful parts of my international major—which was not included in the official course work—was my in-depth study of and practical exams on how to meet exciting local males. Through our experiences, my friends and I found that any girl can become a foreign man magnet. Each time I returned from Europe, I was bombarded with questions about how to meet European men from college girls planning semesters abroad and career women planning vacations across the Atlantic. They returned from these trips with their own terrific man-meeting stories.

This guide, which is chock-full of true stories, begins with a list of the types of single girls who travel abroad and Forty Flirty Tips that work wonders with men. This is followed by the basic varieties of European males you can expect to meet and proven hot spots where you can find them. I changed all names and did a little descriptive camouflaging to avoid potentially embarrassing revelations. This way, no moms will be able to spot their daughters and say, "Oh, I see what she meant when she said she was taking advantage of her time in Europe and really experiencing the culture." Single girls are all about culture . . . especially the cultures of European men!

Don't think my girlfriends and I went around concocting the best place to position ourselves, the best angle at which to stand, and the best way to start a conversation with a European prospect. The tips in this book came from what we did naturally that got the guys and what didn't. So practice them and see what feels natural to you. Most of all, European men want to know that you are having fun. If you truly are, then they will be more attracted to you. Looking like your focus is meeting guys will never lure them in. The more you genuinely have a high time, the more they will want to meet you.

Try on the tips, choose the man-meeting venues that interest you, plan your trip, and go for it. Be sure to take along this guide in case your plans change. Say you are studying in Spain and when you finish classes on a Friday, a friend says, "Let's go to Italy this weekend!" Or you're on your European vacay and get the itch to leave one country and explore another. This happens all the time, and if you have your guide, no problem! Just flip to your new country of interest and scope out the tried-and-true guy-getting hot spots. Tried-and-true is the reason why this guide may have only one hot spot listed in one country and eight in another. It does not mean that one country has better men than another. It means I never want to steer any single girl in the wrong direction so I only included road-tested locations. If you find more, please email me at Katherine@MeetingEuropeanMen.com so we can let others in on the secrets of man-meeting in Europe.

One last note before you dive in: when you see a section titled **Man-Meeting Tidbit**, you can be confident that it will give you the inside scoop on meeting men; a heading beginning with **When . . .** always signals a true man-meeting story; and a **Word to the Wise** heading gives you important information on planning your trip. If you encounter an unfamiliar word or acronym, turn to the handy Slangtionary on page 255.

Types of Single Girls Traveling in Europe

When it comes to female travelers, there are ten general categories. Of course, everyone has unique characteristics, categories can overlap, and many girls head to Europe thinking they are one type and then discover that they are another. What do they all have in common? They want to meet European men!

CDs (Committal Daters)

CDs like having boyfriends. They enjoy being in serious relationships. If these girls are going to be abroad for an extended stay, they feel like they can experience the country best by exclusively dating one European man who can give them an inside look at everything Europe. These types have their boyfriend radars up 24/7. I have a friend who is a Committal Dater all the way. During the rare times when she is not in a serious relationship, she scopes out every hot spot she visits to see if the men are boyfriend material. She has her own personal list of criteria, including everything from a charming personality to being six feet or over, since she is very tall. The men this girl thinks might make good fits she terms "Candidates." The ones who are iffy she calls "Cans." And of the ones who are definite no-goes, she says, "Don't even get a 'C.'" Most CDs are:

Calm. They go about trolling for boyfriends in a manner that seems nonchalant . . . oh, but it is only nonchalant on the outside. They remind me of cheetahs who stealthily examine their prey from a distance and pounce at the opportune moment with lightning speed. But CDs don't pounce on their prospects; they smoothly introduce themselves and start to flirt. The guys are so smitten that they don't know what struck them.

Direct. CDs are direct in a very good way. They're not afraid to say what they think. If a CD faces a roadblock at any stage in a relationship, she confronts it and resolves it right away.

Followers

These girls want to meet the men, but never do. They travel in packs, generally going to Europe with large groups of friends and never breaking away from them the entire time. When their trips end, they wonder why they didn't get the guys. Wonder??? Well, if you never leave your girlfriends' sides, you will never get to be beside the European men.

I have noticed that Followers spend so much time together that they start looking alike—wearing the same style dress, getting the same haircuts, and even taking on the same expressions. Most European men don't want to date a girl who has several clones. Discover yourself! Dare to be a little different. Then get out there and meet the men! In Tip #13, Avoid Prowling in Packs, I will give you the lowdown on why the European guys don't generally chase after Followers.

Fun Seekers

Before I delve into Fun Seekers, I want you to know that every girl I ever traveled to Europe with wanted to have fun, so aspects of this category can overlap with others.

Fun Seekers really do love romance, but they will never go looking for boyfriends. They get into relationships when they find men they really like, but when they don't, they are happy being single. They generally go with the flow, aren't forward or aggressive, and try to make fun absolutely everywhere. Fun Seekers also want others to have a great time. Basically, they care about keeping their fun barometers supercharged.

These types travel to Europe to soak up the culture and enjoy the European men, but they are glad to meet Europeans and other travelers of both sexes and all ages too. If a Fun Seeker finds a guy she wants to go on a date with, great. Then, if she hits it off with him, she will be excited to start steadily dating. And if he is a wonderful fit, she is ready to plunge into a serious relationship. These girls are usually:

Friendly. They smile at people in elevators who they don't even know.

Uninhibited. They tend to do what they feel is best without worrying about what others may think.

Nice. The Fun Seekers I know aren't manipulative. They never want to have fun at the expense of others. Their philosophy is that if they can't get something through hard work and being their true selves, it's not worth getting.

Gift Grabbers

These girls want to be given gifts without giving anything in return. Their sole desire is to be pampered and have things bought for them—the ritzier the better. I have heard Gift Grabbers comparing their success stories. One would say, "I got free drinks from men all night." Another would exclaim, "Well, I got that plus roses." And a third would gloat, "I get that all the time. Jewelry is what I'm going for." When asked about the guys who gave them the gifts, the girls responded, "What guys?" To them, men are just accessories.

Of course, most of us love getting gifts and being treated royally by men, but we genuinely care about those guys and want to be with them. In my opinion, it is wonderful to date men who create romantic surprises, but the key word is "date." Gift Grabbers don't "date"—they "dash." They stay around long enough to get their gifts and then dash on to another guy before the first one realizes what has happened. A Gift Grabber typically stays with one man through an important event, like Valentine's Day or her birthday. Then she collects the goodies and dashes for the door. If a guy wanted to buy a girl presents without developing a relationship with her, he could just give her his credit card. This is clearly not his intent, and getting to know European men is a pleasure, so say "no" to the temptation to be a Gift Grabber!

You may be wondering why I have such negative feelings about Gift Grabbers. Well, my brother was dashed by one, so I have witnessed what it is like for a guy to be on the receiving end. Not fun.

Kissers

The overriding goal of these girls is to kiss a man from every European country they visit. The ways in which they accomplish this vary.

There are two general subcategories: the "Just Get It Done" and the "Must Have Meaning." The "Just Get It Done" girls don't have to date a guy to kiss him. They don't even have to get to know him. In fact, I have even heard these types say that when they run out of time in a particular location and haven't captured the kiss, they will explain their goal to a random prospect and ask him to comply. They remind me of Cub Scouts eagerly collecting merit badges.

The "Must Have Meaning" girls believe that the kiss is not legit if it doesn't have meaning. These types will only kiss men whom they like, have gotten to know, and gone out with. They want a memorable story to accompany the kiss.

NCDs (Non-Committal Daters)

NCDs love to date a variety of European men, but they are not in the committing mood. Dating around is their domain. They can be best described as:

Neutral. It's not that these girls don't care about the men they date. They really do. They're just neutral when it comes to getting emotionally attached. They are not in Europe to have serious relationships.

Charismatic. NCDs have a knack for getting asked out on dates. Their pizzazz just draws the men right in.

Deliberate. These girls are proud to be NCDs. They generally don't hide this fact from the guys they date and typically explain early on that they want to keep the relationship casual. There is a strange phenomenon that I have seen when European men and NCDs mix. The more the girls want to keep things casual, the more the guys want to get serious. I told you these types are full of charismatic charm!

Princess Brides

Like my friend who wanted to find "the one," Princess Brides come to Europe searching for their "happily ever after." They won't settle for "Mr. Right Now" when "Mr. Right" is what they want. They are the Buttercups of Europe. Stopping short of Westleys is out of the question. True love is why they travel abroad, and true love is what they intend to get. Whether a Princess Bride is taking a course, snacking at a café, or skiing in the Alps, she is on the lookout for "the one." She will happily view the beautiful mountains, but that is while viewing the men who are on them.

Samplers

These girls are only in Europe for a short stay . . . maybe even just a one-week vacation from work. They do not have time to seriously date any men or immerse themselves in the culture, so they go for the European Sampler Special. That is something like a little sightseeing, festival-going, hiking, and dancing weaved into making as many European acquaintances as possible. When it comes to having experiences with European men, instead of indulging in a large meal, they sample a variety of dishes.

Sexcapaders

This category is named after my friend the Sexcapader, who framed her European Hookup Map. These types are like Kissers in the sense that they want to experience a guy from every significant European location they visit.

Each Sexcapader goes after getting stars on her map in a unique fashion. My friend preferred hitting up sports bars, especially while games were being played on the TV screens or after big local sporting events. She was sports savvy and could converse with any aficionado about the nuances of the game. Her man-attracting strategy was to get looking cute, push-up bra and all, and head over to the bar with a book, often during the day. Yes, a book. That way the Sexcapader could order a drink and read for however long it took a potential target to walk through the door. Then she would close the book and shoot him one of her prime sports-savvy comments. Surprised that a girl could possibly have such vast knowledge of sports, the guy would take a second look at her, this time noticing her oh-so-sexy outfit, compliments of her natural amenities and the perfect push-up. Mission accomplished! Now all she had to do was figure out where she wanted to get laid.

My friend the Sexcapader explained, "Getting hookup stars is a big responsibility, and girls must understand that big responsibilities can come with some drawbacks." She lamented that, unfortunately, European men don't wine and dine girls they consider to be one-night stands. With her droll sense of humor, she asked me, "Don't they know I'd take some champagne before getting my action? . . . And I wouldn't mind chocolates for the ride home." That is not how it works in the world of in-and-out play. Sexcapaders do ten-yard sprints, while relationship-oriented girls go for marathons.

Social Chairs

These girls are the leaders of the Followers. In every pack there are one or two of them. They set the group schedule, but like their Followers they don't meet the men. Part of the reason for this is because they schedule everything to the last detail, leaving no room for enjoying the guys and seeing what happens spontaneously. Of course it's good to plan, but your plans should be flexible enough so that if a European man suddenly sweeps you off your feet your response isn't, "Sorry, this isn't in the itinerary." This may seem like an unlikely response, but I have witnessed it. One time at a festival, a dashing European man miraculously picked a Follower from the middle of the group. He dared to approach the pack and asked if she and a friend would like to join him and his brother for drinks. The Follower really wanted to, but seeing that the Social Chair was charging forward with the others, she replied, "Oh, I couldn't break away from the group." Come on, just one step! I promise the second one will be easier.

THE BOTTOM LINE

Whatever type of girl you are—or whatever type you become in Europe—you can definitely meet the men. How? By trying out the following flirty tips.

40
FLIRTY
TIPS

How to Prepare for Your Trip

So you're probably thinking, "Bring on those hardcore flirting tips! I'm all about enticing the European men." Well, just like the old adage, "If you don't apply, you won't get the job," if you don't properly plan for your trip, you won't meet the European men. The first six tips tell you how to best plan.

Tip #1:
When to Go—Make Every Day in
Europe Like Your Best Valentine's Day

Really, any time in Europe is mantastic. Check out the attractions and your schedule and choose the dates that suit you. If you plan carefully, this region can make you feel like every day is the perfect Valentine's Day. In fact, if you know that you are going to be beau-less on February 14, don't think of Valentine's Day as SAD (Singles' Awareness Day). Think of it as GLAD (Girls Love Adventure Day).

Grab some friends, map out a European trip, and get out of town for the heart holiday. Make romance the theme. Select some hubs where singles mingle and vow to not be limited to just one valentine. European men want to make women happy. So let them! Have a valentine in England, an *amante* in Spain, a *rakastaja* in Finland, and a *szeretö* in Hungary. And don't stop there! Europe is a great place to date around. If you can't break away for the V-season, then buy yourself some flowers, put on some romantic music, and call a single gals' get-together to plot a future European escape. Preparing for manly foreign attention is just the fix for girls lacking romance on a romantic holiday.

When Miss Scorned Became Miss Hot Tamale

My friend is the poster girl for embarking on adventures with European men when romance is lacking at home. Miss Scorned (as we'll call her) was dumped by her boyfriend for another girl just two weeks before Valentine's Day. To make matters worse, her amour had recently declared that she was perfect for him and that he had never loved anyone as much as he loved her. He proceeded to list all of the romantic festivities he was planning for Valentine's Day. Well, he might have been planning them, but the real question was, for whom? Out of the blue, Mr. Schmuck broke up with her, took up with another girl, and proceeded to flaunt her in front of Miss Scorned. Unfortunately, she couldn't get away from him because they worked for the same company and lived in the same neighborhood. Miss Scorned was devastated. To top it off, she had spent the past year helping to organize a big charity Valentine's ball, and now she had no escort. She felt like she might as well just stamp "UNLOVED" on her forehead.

Miss Scorned made the final arrangements for the ball, grabbed her sister, took a spontaneous trip to Europe, and ordered the

European Sampler Package. They went biking, shopping, or sightseeing every day and dancing every night. The men were very friendly to them and Miss Scorned's sister made a point of letting them know that her travel buddy was "single and ready to mingle," particularly on February 14. Miss Scorned received three dinner invites for that evening. She accepted the one that called for the fanciest attire so she could use the dress she would have worn to the Valentine's ball. She had a wonderful experience and scheduled the other two dinner offers for different nights.

Miss Scorned soon became Miss Spotlight. She gained so much self-confidence in Europe that when she returned home she glowed. The trip gave her the strength to go forward without Mr. Schmuck and ignore his jabs. Many men commented on how good she looked, and some said they wished they had taken her to the Valentine's ball. Well, when the men at home snooze, they lose—to the European gents.

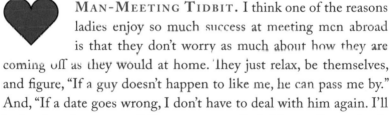 MAN-MEETING TIDBIT. I think one of the reasons ladies enjoy so much success at meeting men abroad is that they don't worry as much about how they are coming off as they would at home. They just relax, be themselves, and figure, "If a guy doesn't happen to like me, he can pass me by." And, "If a date goes wrong, I don't have to deal with him again. I'll be leaving the country." European men find this carefree attitude appealing, so whenever you face a lack of love at home, Europe has the antidote.

When the Romantic Turned Rotten

One of my girlfriends experienced the mirror image of uninhibited self-exploration in a boyfriend. She studied in Greece for a fall/winter semester and had fun meeting many European men, but I want to focus on a fellow traveler with whom she shared an amazing whirl-wind romance. He was from the States like her but they met for the first time in Greece. He was like Eros, the Greek god of love and passion, with his outgoing personality and creative, amorous aura. This was perfect for my friend since she was a lover of everything romantic—love notes, sappy movies where a man tells a woman that he will love only her forever, and visits to love-inspiring locations. In a nutshell, "love" is her favorite word.

The relationship between Miss Love and Mr. Eros caught fire almost instantly and soon became very serious. He crafted amazing love poems for her, and he planned the most enchanting dates and weekend getaways. On a trip to the exquisite Rhodes castle, he vowed to propose to her there one day. Her happiness was his greatest desire. He delighted in surprising her. Before Christmas, she started getting sad as she realized that it would be the first time she couldn't share the holiday with her family. He surprised her with a basket filled with favorite Christmas treats from her hometown so that she could "transport those holiday traditions to Greece."

My friend thought she had met the man she wanted to spend forever with . . . but when they returned to the States, Mr. Eros became Mr. Introvert. He was constantly more concerned about what his friends thought than what would make himself and his girlfriend happy. He no longer surprised her with creative romantic gifts and planned weekend getaways. Apparently he had been an introvert until he visited Greece. There, released from the inhibitions of other people's expectations, he felt free to be adventurous.

Hoping to rekindle the fire her boyfriend had in Europe, Miss Love worked hard to save the relationship. Eventually she realized that she had fallen for Mr. Eros but Mr. Introvert was all she had left. Then, he lost what he had gained in Greece—both the man he really wanted to be and the girl he really wanted to be with.

THE BOTTOM LINE

There is no reason why the wonderful carefree characteristics travelers obtain overseas can't come home with them. In fact, they should. When I say "carefree" I'm not advocating being reckless. I'm suggesting that you free yourself to find yourself. If you have always wanted to join in a jam session but felt embarrassed, Europe is the best place to give it a go. If you feel you are a bad dancer but want to hit up the clubs, Europe is the perfect place to practice your moves. If you have always wanted to go snowboarding but felt inadequate in comparison to your friends, Europe is where you can take lessons and learn. And if you desire to attend an all-night festival but aren't normally a party girl, well Europe has many to choose from. Rest up and give it a whirl!

Through your explorations, you can find both European men and the "you" you've wanted to be.

Tip #2:
Flirting Practice Makes Perfect

I would advise trying as many of the tips in this guide as you can before boarding the plane for your European vacay. We all know that practicing plays before a big sports game scores points. Likewise, practicing the moves that entice European men before going abroad scores dates. It also scores dates at home. In fact, these tips work so well that some of my friends inadvertently got boyfriends before leaving for Europe just by practicing them. This created a pre-trip dilemma they hadn't planned on!

I have noticed, however, that European men—especially those from the southern European countries—are among the quickest to respond to the flirting tips. I saw this principle in practice just last weekend. During the week, I was in LA meeting with a young, eligible male producer. He asked about this guide and had a hard time believing that European men were easier to meet than, say, LA men. He said that if an appealing girl entered an LA club or bar, she "could have nine out of ten guys there." I countered that although she may be able to have them, she might have to work harder to get to know them than she would with many European men.

That weekend, I was excited to be put on the list for one of the top Los Angeles clubs. In LA, it is very difficult to get into the best ones. They have enormously long lines and most of the people standing in them never get inside. Basically, you have to know someone who knows a club promoter who can put you on the list . . . or be a celebrity. I was fortunate to have a girlfriend who is so appealing that the last time she went clubbing, the promoter gave her his number and said to call anytime she wanted in. OK, obviously she is pretty ridiculously appealing. You would have thought that when we went clubbing she would have been swarmed by several guys. Well, she only got the "sev" in several. Most of the guys we met were charming but a little reserved.

That same weekend, at dusk, I was in Beverly Hills crossing the street from the business district to the park when some eye-catching men stopped to wave at me. Mind you, at that moment I was no traffic-stopper. Whereas at the club I had been dolled-up to the nines, here on the street I was in workout attire with messy hair and no makeup. One of the guys kept waving and smiling, trying to make a connection across the rush hour traffic. When I reached the park, the men introduced themselves. Guess what? They were visiting from Paris. We chatted and had a great time until I had to leave to get ready for the evening. They wanted me to join them, but I couldn't.

They insisted on giving me their contact info and sincerely said that if I visit Paris they would love to show me around.

So, if you master the flirting tips in this guide when you are at home, you will surely find success in Europe.

Tip #3:
Don't Let a Tight Budget
Cut You Out of European Fun

If finances are not an issue for you, skip this tip, but if they are, read on. You can't meet the men if you can't make the trip. I have two adventurous friends who just went abroad and worked out their finances when they arrived. I don't recommend this approach, but it worked for them. One girl paid for her vacay by playing the piano at bars, restaurants, and clubs in every city she visited. The other girl used her credit cards. She had just taken the bar exam and landed a good job, but having just finished law school and spent six weeks studying for the bar, she had no money. She reasoned that this was one of the rare times in her life when she could take a vacation with no obligations. To her, the trip was well worth the payments afterward. Clearly, both of these girls used creative budgeting skills, but there are many ways to finance your European escape without having to play the piano or max out your credit cards.

Semester Abroad. Most universities offer a semester abroad, and the only difference in price from a semester at home is usually the airfare. Student discounts are also offered at many European establishments, especially for entertainment. If you have the choice of staying in the dorms or with a family, the family route is much cheaper. For one flat meal-plan fee, your host will usually provide all the food you will ever need and much more. This typically costs less than a university cafeteria plan—not to mention the fact that those families cook amazing meals. They can also help you learn the language, give you inside information about entertainment in the area, and introduce you to European men.

Staying in Dorms on Vacations and Business Trips. Even if you are not a student, check out the college dorms if you are traveling in the summer. Many universities rent out rooms then because enrollment is low. While I was at the London School of Economics, I sometimes ran into businessmen staying in my dorm. They said the lodging there was the best-kept secret in the city. One man came every year for a month and bought the meal plan. Not only were those dorms economical, they were comfortable and centrally located. He had maid service, clean towels, and in-house dining, just like the fancy hotels but at a fraction of the cost. There was a subway station and a cash machine around the corner, plus stores and businesses across the street and an Internet café only a block away.

Airfare Discounts. With regard to airfare, I'd advise adding websites for the airlines and discount travel agencies to your favorites and checking fares to your preferred destination once a day. Without any notice, ticket prices can drastically change. If you get in on the low end, you can save hundreds of dollars.

Students have long had the advantage of getting discounts through student travel agencies like STA Travel and Student Universe. Recently, these companies have begun offering the same discounts to nonstudents.

Bargain Seasons. For those who are not in school, there are several more cost-cutting options. Fall is usually the most economical season to schedule your European vacay. Plus, the weather is milder and there are fewer visitors. And don't think an economic slump is cause to put off your trip. Travel sales and discounts generally improve when economies dip.

Ask for a Refrigerator. When booking your hotel or hostel, ask if the lodging has a refrigerator that guests can use. This is a great money-saver. When I was studying at the London School of Economics the restaurants in my neighborhood were very pricey—like at least twelve pounds a meal. You can get an amazing dress at one of the coveted Euro flea markets for that price! Luckily, my dorm had a community refrigerator. I bought food at the market and packed my own lunches. When I was in a time bind, I could whip up something quick and healthy for breakfast or a before-class snack. Fruits, vegetables, and sliced meats were sold at the markets in reasonably priced packages that lasted an entire week. By buying my food this way, each meal cost less than one pound, so I had more money to hit the town and meet the men.

Follow the Flirting Tips in This Guide. Many of the tips in this guide will actually help you cut costs. For example, knowing how to act while strutting through Leicester Square can get you megadiscounted club passes (see London Hot Spot on page 138).

When the Sexcapader Locked Up Her Star Map

You will find that European men do not let budgetary restrictions stop them from entertaining you. Those with lavish budgets will take you to nice restaurants and premium entertainment. Those with tight budgets will plan equally romantic dates like a bike ride through the countryside with a stop for ice cream at a quaint little village or an evening at a festival on the beach.

My friend the Sexcapader enjoyed many European men, but her favorite was a student on a very tight budget. She was studying in France and made weekend visits to different countries in her quest to add stars to her hookup map. One weekend in Berlin she met a charming German man at a district of bars and lounges known as the singles' alley for college students. They had amazing chemistry, shared the same interests, and were even studying the same subjects.

For once, she locked her star map in the drawer and spent the entire visit building a relationship.

Her German amour was working his way through school, and money was extremely tight. He couldn't even afford a car. When my girlfriend left Berlin, she was falling for him but thought that her weekend would remain nothing but a great memory. She was wrong. Mr. G called saying that he couldn't stop thinking about her and would find a way to visit. How would he without money? Last time I checked, it still doesn't grow on trees in Germany. But when a European man wants to see you, he will find a way. Mr. G surfed hitchhiking sites and rode with six different strangers to reach my friend in France. They spent his weeklong school break together.

When she left Lyon for home, the smitten Sexcapader took a puddle jumper from there to Munich for a short layover. Her Berlin man had come down with a severe case of love-itis. You know, it's practically an epidemic there. He helped a friend study for an exam in exchange for borrowing his car. Then Mr. G drove over five hours in the hope of getting to see the object of his desire for five minutes before she boarded her next plane. Don't you just adore those romantics?

So never think that a tight budget is cause for cutting out European men!

Tip #4:
Double-Check Before You Check In

Double-checking before you check in increases the chances of enjoying your trip. One of my friends failed to double-check before checking in to a Swiss ski resort that she had heard was a winter wonderland. Unfortunately, when she arrived there wasn't enough snow for good skiing, much less attracting European men. What was she left with? A snowless, manless ski trip.

When Miss Angelic Spent the Night in a Brothel

Another friend failed to double-check her lodging and ended up unwittingly staying in a brothel. This girl is a total angel. She is the intelligent but innocent type who always follows the rules and never gets in trouble. She and a friend wanted to take a vacation to London. Miss Angelic usually researches everything, but this trip was spur-of-the-moment and she had to put her researching talent into a bioscience paper. Not only did she not have much preparation time, she didn't have much money. She booked what she thought was the cheapest London hotel and couldn't believe her good fortune at finding it.

Miss Angelic and her friend arrived in the city and took the bus to where she was told the "hotel" would be, but nothing was there. When they asked the bus driver for further directions he replied, "Are you sure you want to be dropped off at that address?" My friend explained that she didn't need to stay in an expensive hotel and live like the Royal Family to have a great London experience. The bus driver looked at her like, "What hotel?" He reluctantly agreed to take the girls to their lodging even though it was not on his route . . . or any driver's. It was in an isolated area. The "hotel" looked more like a strange house. It had a living room filled with sleazy men, a lot of little rooms nearby, and an invisible sign at the entrance warning, "Leave anything angelic on the doorstep."

When my friend booked the room, the proprietor assumed she wanted to make a little ho-dough on her European trip, so she quoted the standard working girl's rental fee. The madam must have realized the error when she met the girls, but Miss Angelic did not fully understand her position until the next morning. The girls arrived too late at night to find a real hotel. Without explaining the situation, the madam showed them to their room and made sure they were not solicited by clients. They were lucky that she did. In the morning they realized that the lock on their door did not work. Many of the men waiting in the living room were only partly dressed. All of them offered to buy the girls breakfast. Do you think maybe they wanted something in return?

Well, it was a London trip to remember but not the type that Miss Angelic had hoped for. She could have found a great deal on a hotel or hostel if she had double-checked before checking in.

The Vanishing Bar. I only put top-notch guy-getting venues in this guide and triple-checked everything. Still, I realize that conditions at any given place can change at any given time. For example, one of the most popular European man-meeting haunts in Italy closed abruptly. This was a gem in a teeming college town. Students from all over Italy filed in to receive their dating degrees. The same matchmaking waiters worked there every day. They even had a bar dog. When I made my final fact-check I found that this desirable destination had suddenly vanished, dog and all! Rumor has it that they are just refurbishing. That was the only vanishing act in this entire book, so you're on firm ground here, but double-checking hot spots is wise and I've made it easy for you to do so by giving you the contact information for each one.

Tip #5:
Be Safe

Once you have researched and background checked your route and destination before heading off, it is important to take appropriate safety precautions. Then, refuse to ruin your trip with worry. My friends and I enjoyed every city we visited and avoided danger.

It's in the Bag. Many travel books advise you to wear a pouch hung on a strap around your neck and stuffed into your blouse to protect your cash and credit cards. Although this will fulfill the intended purpose, it will keep away the guys as well as the pickpockets. Your sexy strapless gown just won't look the same with a money bulge in the bodice. And the string tying it around your neck will never pass as a necklace. You can be both safe and trendy if you get a cute clutch with a short strap and keep it tucked under your arm at all times. I safely wore my little beige one all over Europe, from the festivals to the flea markets.

If you need a bigger bag to carry things like maps and sunglasses, some friends recommend hipster bags with straps that sling diagonally across your body. They bought theirs in Europe. The bags are stylish, let your arms stay free, and remain safely close by. Hipster bags come in a variety of sizes, some with smaller compartments for wallets, cell phones, and keys. This may not sound to you like a flirty tip, but you won't meet European men if you get your passport stolen and spend your vacation at the embassy!

Safety in Numbers. I know girls who only feel safe traveling with a friend, others who will travel alone but meet up with friends in different European cities, and two gutsy girlfriends who just take off by themselves whenever they want a break, regardless of whether they can rendezvous with someone. Neither of them has been in an unsafe situation but they are extremely careful about where and when they go, and they will not visit a country alone unless the trip is well planned and they know the language.

When Emma Was Offered Sixty Camels

When you are traveling with a companion, choose that person wisely. We all know friends who are great fun but have a talent for getting into trouble. This principle also applies to family members. One of the most entertaining stories I've heard proves this point. Every female knows that in her dad's mind she will always be his little girl, whether she is three or thirty-three. Especially when it comes to teenagers, parents can get pretty concerned about sending girls over the ocean with friends. I have been traveling by myself since the age of fourteen and every time I leave for Europe my dad still thinks he should be my bodyguard. Well, my friend traveled with her bodyguard dad and despite his good intentions, he was the one who placed her in jeopardy!

This girl is beautiful and innocently casts an empowering spell on men. Let's call her Emma because she reminds me of the character in the book. Like that heroine, my girlfriend does not realize that she is attractive. Emma has luscious eyelashes that extend forever. When I complimented them once, she replied, "Oh it's just my Maybelline mascara." That's Emma for you. When she was eighteen, her parents visited a European part of Istanbul to buy rugs for their house. Of course, the thirty-year-old rug seller would have to have the major hots for Emma. Older men are in, but Emma felt that at her age a guy over a decade older was too old.

Emma's parents bonded with Rug Seller. He invited the three of them to dine at his restaurant. After eating, watching whirling dervishes, and smoking hookahs, Rug Seller challenged Emma's dad to a game of backgammon. Her dad said that if he won, Rug Seller would have to give him a free rug. Rug Seller replied that if he won, he got Emma. Yikes! Well, you can guess who won . . . Rug Seller. He proceeded to tell Emma's parents that he was the perfect suitor for her. He claimed his assets included a yacht and over one million US dollars in addition to his rug business, restaurant, and some hotels. He even offered sixty camels for her hand. And I thought Johnny Lingo was generous!

Emma's dad thought Rug Seller was kidding and suggested he take her out on the town. Do you think maybe he had smoked a little too much hookah? Emma engaged in what she described as "hand-to-hand combat," fighting off Rug Seller's advances throughout the evening. She was relieved to return home, certain that her problems with him were over. Wrong! Just two weeks later, her suitor showed up at her American home calling Emma's parents "Future Father- and Mother-in-Law." When is the wedding? Uh, never! I know Emma well. If left to her own devices she would never have gotten herself in this predicament.

From her story, you can also see that you don't want to give a foreign man who you don't know well a way to track you down. Until you are sure that you can trust a guy, I'd play it safe. It seems like common sense to not get into a car with or go back to the home of a man you just met, but I have friends who did it in Europe. The male charm there was so strong that it obscured their perspective. Looking back, they asked me to warn single girls that losing control can lead to scary situations. Even my girlfriend who put the hookup stars on her European map feels that she took too many risks. She was nineteen at the time. Now that she is older, she says that if she had it to do again she would be more careful.

STDs Aren't the European Souvenirs Single Girls Seek. Also, it may seem obvious, but sleeping with random men can be dangerous. I have many types of girlfriends from saints to sluts. I love them all. The Sexcapader left caution at home. Another friend had every guy who wanted to get intimate take an STD test. In fact, she had them take two in case the first was faulty. And the men accommodated her quirky request. A third girlfriend confided that she loved kissing and chose to only go that far. I don't want to linger on unpleasant topics, so whatever you choose to do with the men in Europe, just be careful.

Finally, as with your hometown hotties, only stay with guys who make you feel good. This was my motto and I had only good experiences with European men.

Tip #6:
Let the Memories Live On

When your plane takes off from Europe and heads for home, the only tangible reminders of your foreign romantic relationships will be your pictures. Having the right camera is crucial. The first few times I traveled overseas, my camera was top-of-the-line in quality but so big that it would in no way fit inside my cute clutch. It was also heavy. Every time I took it with me, I felt like I was lugging around a weight. So what happened? It stayed parked in my room and I came home from my vacation almost photoless. During my next several European trips, I thought I was wise by bringing a tiny, trendy camera. There was no problem tucking it into my clutch and it was quite the fashion statement, but again pictures were not a large part of my vacay. My camera was so fragile that finicky was its forte. In steamy clubs and moist climates its images were often a blur.

I'd advise getting one of the Olympus Stylus Tough cameras. They are known for being shockproof, waterproof, and freeze-proof, making them the ideal choice for the active girl. Your Olympus can go with you anywhere, from a candlelit beach dinner to skiing to basking in the sun. Want to wade in the ocean waves? Bring your Olympus. With it, you can even take high-quality underwater pictures and movies. Say you get so mesmerized by your European stud that you drop your cam five feet. No problem. Just pick it back up and click another pic. These cameras vary in price, so go to www.olympus america.com and see what fits your budget. In fact, some of the cutest colors come in some of the most reasonable versions.

How to Mentally Prepare for Success

Tip #7:
Commit to Self-Fulfilling Prophecy

Now that you have your cute clutch or hipster bag and trustworthy camera, before stepping into man-land you need to have self-fulfilling prophecy on your side. Some say this is hocus-pocus—but it's definitely not! If you believe that you can make European male magic, then you will be able to cast your spell on almost any man. However, if you believe that you are guy-jinxed, book your flight back home because you will be left alone. Self-fulfilling prophecy is way more important than natural beauty.

When Plain Jane Lured in the Lads

Take my two girlfriends for example—let's call them Elena and Jane. The first one had jaw-dropping features. She could have doubled for Catherine Zeta-Jones as Elena Montero in *The Mask of Zorro* with her perfect long hair, glowing eyes, and amazing curvy figure. Did this get her anywhere with the European gents? No. Before traveling overseas, she had been devoured by several womanizers. She was bitter and proclaimed that her bad luck wouldn't change in Europe. She was right. Instead of giving off an optimistic vibe, she oozed gloom. No dates were in her horoscope.

My other friend was a plain Jane. Even with the help of a top Hollywood stylist and ample amounts of mascara, she was at best a five. This didn't stop her. She went out with confidence and charisma. On any given night, at least three guys genuinely told her that she was enchanting. Her date card was always full.

THE BOTTOM LINE

Any girl can use self-fulfilling prophecy to her advantage. I like getting to know different kinds of people with different backgrounds and interests, so I have a wide variety of girl-friends. All of them found success with European males, from the beauty pageant winner to the "Why mess with makeup?" outdoors-lover, from the competitive athlete to the never-entered-the-gym bookworm, and from the science scholar to the professional burlesque dancer. They all had self-fulfilling prophecy on their side.

When the Burlesque Dancer Fell for the Italian Stallion

When you commit to this philosophy, you take on a guy-attracting glow. Since you never know when and where you will meet European men, it is crucial to cultivate this state of mind even when guys aren't around. I have this friend who is a bundle of joy. She looks like an adorable blonde Kewpie doll, with her short pixie hairdo and cute clothing. Let's call her Betsey, because she is like a live Betsey Johnson ad all done up with her scarves, boots, and fabulous flirty dresses.

Betsey performs in a professional burlesque troupe that travels to exciting destinations like Europe. Don't you just feel bad for her? Yeah right! One night she went out with her girlfriend Lacey. They didn't find any men, but that didn't put a damper on Betsey's attitude. She had a blast "getting down" on the dance floor—and with her burlesque training you know she can really get down. Even though she didn't meet an enthralling European guy that evening, she did make a new girlfriend, Carmen. Making girlfriends can often lead to meeting men, especially when the girlfriend has a European boyfriend with male friends. This was the case with Carmen. Well, Betsey, Carmen, and Lacey were on a picture-taking high that night . . . posing and clicking 'til the clubs closed down. Carmen put up a picture of Betsey on her bulletin board. When Carmen's Italian boyfriend and his dashing friend Arnaldo dropped by, Arnaldo couldn't take his eyes off Betsey's picture. Carmen planned to meet up with Betsey the following night and invited her boyfriend and Arnaldo to come along.

In her normal mode, Betsey is always full of energy and always has something funny to say, but when she was introduced to Arnaldo, she was frozen and speechless. He was way too cute for words. Once she realized that she hadn't lost her voice, they got along great. When an obnoxious guy started coming on to Betsey, Arnaldo came to her rescue and suggested that the two of them go off alone. Suave move, super stud! That was just the beginning. They got along so well that

Arnaldo got a work visa to Betsey's hometown in the US. They had a sexy summer romance and then he had to return to Italy.

Was that all? OK, maybe not. About a month ago, Arnaldo sincerely told Betsey that he loved her. She explained that she couldn't say those words back to him or she would get too attached. He just kept saying them to her anyway, proclaiming, "If you feel something you should not hold back . . . just say it and don't think about the consequences." Before Betsey knew what struck, she was saying "I love you" to him. Too late to not get attached! Betsey is totally smitten and counting down the days until Arnaldo visits her again . . . only forty-one left.

In the meantime, Arnaldo sends Betsey the most romantic emails with adorations like, "The beach is melancholy without you." How could you not fall for this guy? Betsey says she has locked in her heart two philosophies from Arnaldo: "There is always time to be romantic. No matter how busy life gets, you can pull your lover aside for a quick kiss." And, "In my country, men take pride in the fact that we are called Italian stallions. I won't let you down." Arnaldo definitely never lets Betsey down. Right now, it's 8 PM in Betsey's time zone. She only has four more hours until the Arnaldo Visit Countdown hits forty days. Is someone maybe a little love struck?

You never know when or where you will meet European men so, like Betsey, always believe in self-fulfilling prophecy and keep that guy-attracting glow going for you. I have one last story just in case you're not quite sold on its power.

When the Girls Charmed Their Way onto the Guest List

A friend of mine visited Spain for the weekend with a few girlfriends. It just so happened that while they were there, one of the swanky champagne companies was hosting an extravagant fiftieth anniversary event. There was a strict guest list with a bouncer to make sure that no uninvited revelers snuck in. As the girls passed the entrance to the party, it looked so inviting that they asked the bouncer about it. Of course, this was delivered with their million-dollar smiles. He slipped them in the door to learn about the event firsthand. To this day my friend isn't quite sure how they scored an invite, but she believes the adventurous, carefree sparkle in their eyes had something to do with it. That night was their most enchanting European memory, complete with a parade of oversized punch bowls filled with champagne and dancers wearing beyond-gorgeous sequined corsets—not to mention the stunning European men eager to meet them.

Believing in self-fulfilling prophecy is often what lights the fireworks in relationships with European men. So go out there and experiment. Don't worry if some of your plans don't exactly work out, because the times that they do and what you will learn about yourself from them will be more than worth it!

How to Wear What
Gets the Guys

Looking appropriate is important for meeting European men no matter what activities or types of guys interest you. The following tips apply to every girl in every situation.

Tip #8:
Opposites Attract

We all know that girls who are not from England or Sweden love to listen to the Brits' charming accents and gaze into the Swedes' stunning blue eyes; likewise, many European TDHs (tall dark and handsome) are attracted to women with features distinctly different from theirs. For example, if you are vacationing where the locals have dark hair, the secret to becoming the center of attention is getting highlights. But be sure to make them look natural. I realize that platinum blonde with dark roots and dark hair underneath is a look that many find sexy, but it can be a European male repellent, along with skunk stripes and grow-outs. When I studied in Madrid one of my bleached-blonde girlfriends was absolutely stunning and anxious to impress the Spanish *hombres*, but they acted uninterested. In fact, many commented on her dark roots and said she was only pretending to be blonde. Don't commit this man-meeting faux pas.

When I Had My Scarlett O'Hara Fix

I learned firsthand how much opposites attract at the acclaimed Madrid nightclub Kapital, where my fantasy of being a European Scarlett O'Hara came true. If you are a female with light hair, Kapital is an absolute must-go. It is a gorgeous Spanish club with equally gorgeous European men. My two closest clubbing girlfriends in Spain could have been mistaken for Spaniards—both have striking dark features. One is half Latino and the other is Greek. I, on the other hand, am very fair with auburn hair and green eyes. I was on a dance/cheer team for Vanderbilt University. Well, we basically just shook our pom-poms and butts. Most of my teammates were light blondes, so I was referred to as one of the few "brunettes." I may have been considered a brunette there, but I was considered a blonde at Kapital in comparison to all the Spaniards.

My friends and I went and re-went to Kapital, and there were always about four guys per girl. So awesome! But I don't think I ever saw another girl without brown eyes and dark brown hair. There was no way that I couldn't stick out at this landmark. Despite the fact that my two Spanish-looking girlfriends were very appealing, let's face it, Kapital was a blonde girl's paradise.

Ever since I read *Gone with the Wind* in high school, I wanted to experience the lavish Twelve Oaks picnic from Scarlett's perspective . . . surrounded by all of the eligible men, having the Tarleton twins vying for my attention, and Rhett Butler (got to love him) plotting to use his best moves to seduce me. Most of the guys at Kapital have the features and coloring of Rhett, so what better place to become a European Scarlett O'Hara? There I was, literally manopolized by Spanish *guapos*. Guys were constantly cutting each other off to ask me to dance while multiple men were offering me drinks. It felt unreal.

There are seven floors in this club. When I moved from floor to floor, the guys followed. My girlfriends thought it was so funny. They started counting how many men danced with me in an evening. Each time we went to Kapital, they challenged me to up the number. The last time I *fiesta*-ed at the club, I didn't dance with a single European male for longer than one song without another one cutting in. Two of my favorites were José and Antonio. One would dance with me, the other would cut in, and then the first would cut back in. Whenever another man tried to approach, they both stared him down. Well, this cycle kept going until finally the two guys turned to me and declared, "It's up to you. Who do you want to be with?" José proceeded to list off his credentials and then Antonio tried to up him. I couldn't get a word in edgewise with these two going back and forth. When the manager approached, I thought there was going to be trouble. Instead, he pushed the gents aside and showed me that he had "way better moves than those two men."

I wish I could say that I always get the Scarlett O'Hara treatment, but definitely not! Kapital is the place where light-haired girls shine among the dashing dark-haired Spaniards. I told my other light-haired girlfriends about this haunt. They visited and had equally wonderful experiences. As for my lovely Latin-looking girlfriends, they had to go someplace like Sweden where blondes were in the majority to get their Scarlett O'Hara fix. So if your hair is anywhere in the blonde family, why just dream about the Twelve Oaks ball when you can go to Kapital?

Tip #9:
Dress It Up

Dressing it up is probably the most important tip for inciting initial male intrigue. This doesn't mean looking red carpet ready at all times. And "dressing up" has completely different meanings depending on the activities you engage in. Wearing a designer dress is obviously only going to attract bewildered stares when taking a hike, going to the beach, or even attending a festival. But no matter what your plans, you can flaunt an appropriately flattering outfit.

And by the way, even at dressy events a designer frock is never needed when dressing to impress. If you can afford that luxury, go for it, but if not, no problem. Any girl on any budget can dress it up for travel. I didn't want to risk bringing my best clothes to Europe in case my bags got lost or stolen. So I did some pre-trip shopping at outlet stores during their red-tag sales (75 percent off last-marked price) for my basic travel attire. You don't need to pop for a travel wardrobe worth hundreds of dollars when you can model guy-getting outfits with only one zero at the end of each price tag, or less. Plus, if you buy your basic wardrobe all at once, like I did, you can coordinate colors so that you take an absolute minimum of shoes, bags, and accessories . . . which conveniently leaves more room in your suitcase for souvenirs.

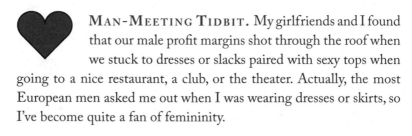 MAN-MEETING TIDBIT. My girlfriends and I found that our male profit margins shot through the roof when we stuck to dresses or slacks paired with sexy tops when going to a nice restaurant, a club, or the theater. Actually, the most European men asked me out when I was wearing dresses or skirts, so I've become quite a fan of femininity.

When We Dressed Our Way into the Swanky Restaurant

A prime example of the power of dresses occurred when my favorite girly trio went to one of the oldest restaurants in Europe. The food was famous for being delish and the décor was one of a kind. Reservations were required days in advance. Before heading out, we all put on fun, flirty dresses and fluffed out our hair as if we were preparing for a *Vogue* photo shoot. But we forgot one little detail—the reservation. I thought my friend had called in and my friend thought that I had. When we arrived at the restaurant, we were informed that there was no room for us. We sadly turned to leave, but the maître d'—who I might add was off-the-radar hot—stopped us, saying, "Please wait for one moment. You got all dressed up and everything. Let me see what I can do." An additional table was set up in the prime location. As he led us to it he explained, "The band normally plays here, but tonight we rearranged things a bit."

I've been hooked on dresses ever since! You can let them work all their wonders. But you might want to resist the temptation of wearing your four-inch stilettos with them. In some of the most charming European locations, the streets are covered in cobblestones. Being able to walk comfortably is very important.

Word to the Fashion Wise. These days there are a number of shoe brands to choose from that are reasonably priced and comfortable. I don't want to sound like an ad, but I have found that Söfft has really appealing and foot-friendly heels. Once, at a crowded festival where the cab companies could not dispatch cars, I walked for ninety minutes in a pair of Söffts and suffered no blisters. For a great, but more pricey option, I'd recommend Cole Haan with Nike Air. I wore a pair once for twelve hours. They were so comfortable that it almost felt like I was in my sneakers the whole time. OK, my commercial is over. Seriously, try them out!

When Miss Athletic Didn't Attract the Buff Hunks

I realize that some of you may not like wearing dresses, or may even think *yuck!* at the thought of getting gussied-up. If you are more of a nature-lovin' chick, dressing it up still works. I have a friend who is an amazing athlete. She backpacked through Europe. Men were not in short supply, but she didn't get to connect with any of them. One of her problems was that she brought all her old, ratty clothes. Holes were the theme of her wardrobe, and I'm not talking about stylish, strategically located rips. She planned on dumping everything in Europe at the end of her vacay. I'm not saying that she didn't have a wonderful experience hiking and climbing through luscious land-scapes, but the entire time she was missing an up-close-and-personal look at some other impressive views—European men. Her trip would have been even more wonderful if she had been escorted by a buff outdoor hunk.

When Miss Unathletic Attracted all the Buff Hunks

Another friend of mine is not athletic but always up for anything. She wanted to try climbing in Europe, but her strength was in her fashion sense, not her muscles. She looked like someone posing for an engaging REI spread in her cute, coordinated clothes. What do you know? She had her own personal male European trainer offering assistance every moment. She couldn't climb above ten feet on her own, but she was the first to reach the top of the mountain in the sport of man-meeting.

When I Hitchhiked in My Cute Clothes

My brother is an outdoor-sports expert, so I have been around a lot of these types of athletes. Many times he has tried to entice me with the thrill of climbing, but I'm not a natural at hanging off of rocks and ice. In fact, when I just hiked up a steep hill with friends in

Europe—or should I say attempted to hike—I almost passed out and had to resort to hitchhiking. An extremely appealing guy in a jeep gave us a ride the rest of the way up. It was going up that was hard, but I really wanted to see the castle at the top of the cliff. I had faith that the trip down would work itself out. I learned from this experience that being rescued by a seductive male loses a certain amount of charm when your face is a deep shade of purple. No amount of cute clothes will cure that. So if you're like me, while you're getting your wardrobe together, consider some training . . . or stay on flat ground during your trip.

 MAN-MEETING TIDBIT. From being around my brother and his friends, I know that girls who are true outdoors babes have great bods, but many of them don't capitalize on their goods. While hiking, they usually wear long shorts or Capris that chop the impressive lines of their toned legs. Hello! If you've got it, flaunt it. Online and at many sporting goods stores, you can find butt-hugging shorts or flattering pants that show off your curves. Most hardcore sports tops are kind of plain. If you have a six-pack, don't just wear a shapeless V-neck tee. Many of my fit girlfriends spice up their plain tops by doing things like cutting the side seams all the way up to the armpits. Then they put little horizontal slits along the seams and tie knots all the way down, revealing snippets of skin. If you really want to get the chaps revved up, wear a brightly colored sports bra underneath your tee and cut diagonal slashes on the front of it. Remember a little skin is in when you dress it up!

Tip #10:
Go Shopping

Although the locals like your unique look, they also want to feel that you make an effort to fit into their culture. When you arrive, go shopping and get some outfits that reflect the foreign fashion. I did this in Spain with great results. At the Running of the Bulls in Pamplona, my girlfriends and I wore the traditional white clothing and red scarves and sashes in honor of San Fermín. While painting the town red afterward, we were rewarded with serenades by groups of Spanish *caballeros* who were honored by our attire. The natives clearly felt a kinship with us. We had invitations to more dinners than we could eat. Romance is in the air, or as they say in Spain, "Se siente el romance en el aire!"

When I Had My Craziest Spain Experience

At a car race on my first trip to Spain, I wore the Formula 1 shirt of one of the native racers and an official took me into the VIP section, which was a rose garden with a prime close-up view of the track. That was the beginning of my craziest Spain experience. I even got to meet some of the racers, but not my favorite one. In fact, during the extravaganza I didn't know he existed, even though in the minds of many he was my "Spanish boyfriend." OK, you are probably really confused. Let me start at the beginning.

Everyone at the car race spoke only Spanish. At the time, I hardly knew the language. I had my zoo animals and colors down really well, but no one said those words. When I bought the Formula 1 shirt, I did not realize that the patches on it were of sponsors for Fernando Alonso, a famous Spanish car racer. I didn't even know who Fernando Alonso was—shame on me. Apparently I didn't know a lot of things about car racing, but I wanted to join in the spirit of the event, look cute, and stay cool in the heat, so I wore my miniskirt, adorable shoes, and new racing shirt. When I got to the event, I realized that no one else—and I mean *no one*—wore a skirt of any kind, especially not a miniskirt. It was too late to go home and change. In fact, it was impossible with the blocked-off roads and huge crowds.

None of my friends wanted to attend the race so I tried to buy a single ticket. I soon learned that the attraction had been sold out for almost a year, even though I didn't know about it until I saw the barricades going up the day before. The official who took me to the VIP section said that one ticket was being held in case someone important came to town at the last minute. He gave it to me and made me promise that I wouldn't tell anyone who he was. If you want to get into the VIP section for the next race, I'm sorry, my lips are sealed . . . What official?

Everyone in the VIP section was either a relative or girlfriend of one of the racers, except me in my miniskirt and Fernando's shirt. The gated rose garden was breathtaking and only about ten feet from the cars. It was like watching a car race from a secret garden. At first, everything seemed relatively normal. I loved watching the cars zoom by up close—especially the red ones. After a couple of hours, I temporarily left the VIP section to buy some lunch, and newsmen with cameras followed me. They asked me lots of questions in Spanish. Wanting to be cordial and not understanding a word they said I answered "sí" to everything and told them how much I loved the red cars.

After lunch, I returned to the rose garden and continued enjoying the cars and cute male attendees. When the race was over, I was introduced to some of the French racers, and then I started for home. Flocks of people, photographers, and cameramen followed me. Several asked for my autograph. All of them were yelling and trying to get my attention. I was frightened, so I called my mom in America. What exactly did I think she could do half a world away? Not sure. But when a girl is in trouble, Mom seems like a good resource. She suggested that I dart into a small business, dash out the back door, and hurry home. I did, and at first I thought I had lost my entourage, but they caught up with me. Seeing my predicament, a fireman offered me a ride home in his truck.

The next morning, I thought everything was back to normal, but I was wrong. On the way to school, more people stopped me asking questions in Spanish that I did not understand. They all said one word over and over again. It was "Alonso." I didn't have my Spanish dictionary with me so I couldn't look it up . . . as if it would be in there under "hot car racer"! When I arrived at class my teacher said—in English, thank goodness—"So I hear you are Fernando Alonso's girlfriend." Fernando who? I soon learned that I had answered "sí" to the question of whether I was dating Fernando. The cameras that had been following me were from the local news.

I don't think you have to worry about inciting the same pandemonium when you go to Europe and wear the native fashion, but you will never have a boring trip. So ladies, go shopping. Then gentlemen, start your engines!

Caveat. If you do attend a car race in Spain, never say, "Estoy excitada por los manejadores." *Excitada* does sound like *excited*, but it's not. The phrase actually is the equivalent of saying, "I'm sexually aroused by the car racers." I learned that at the race, too. I was just trying to pick up the language and make small talk with a nice European man. I did leave an impression, but not the one I was going for. If you want to express your excitement about the car racers say, "Estoy emocionada por los manejadores." I know it sounds like you are confessing to being emotional, but you aren't. It is one of those deceptively tricky phrases.

Similarly, if you get hot watching the car race out in the sun, in some places you should not say, "Estoy caliente." I realize that if you look up the word *caliente* in a Spanish dictionary, the first definition often says "warm," but in some regions you are not saying, "I'm warm." Instead you are declaring, "I'm sexually excited." "I'm hot" is "Tengo calor." How do I know this? Oh, another one of my mistakes!

How to Travel

Knowing how to travel involves way more than putting liquids in a plastic quart bag before going through the metal detector at the airport. Knowing who and who not to travel with is critical in attracting European men.

Tip #11:
Leave Homeboys at Home

I know how important it is in life to keep your options open, but to really do Europe right, your only male options should be Europeans. Many girls try to hang on to their hometown honeys. Placing each of your feet in a different world will never work. Trust me. I've tried it.

Emailing Home Weekly from an Internet Café Is Perfect. The first time that I went abroad, I had been seeing this guy from school. We were at that open relationship stage. I let him know that I would be spending the summer away, but hoped to get together when I returned. He asked to stay in contact. I didn't have a computer with me, my pricey foreign phone was used sparingly, and he thought writing letters seemed so old-fashioned. I compromised. We emailed each other once a week when I hit up an Internet café. It worked wonderfully. I didn't let the flame in that relationship burn out, yet I wasn't tethered to my life so many miles away. I had complete freedom to explore the enthralling European male possibilities all around me.

Daily Contact with Hometown Honeys Cuts Out Euro Men. So, I'm definitely not advising you to sever home ties. But don't get glued to your Skype, buy an unlimited calling plan, or sign up for twenty-four-hour Internet access. You will get so involved with your homeboy that you might as well have never left home. I made this mistake on my second trip overseas. I was in that odd phase where I wasn't technically the girlfriend, but my American man still got jealous when I went out with other guys. At the beginning of my European trip, we stayed in close touch. Between talking every day, emailing excessively, and even sending messages via snail mail, I didn't have enough time away from my hometown hottie to experience Europe's masculine wonders.

My home tie asked every night if I was seeing any of the local men. Unfortunately the answer was no. And my European love meter stayed parked on zero until after three weeks, when I finally explained to my distant distraction, "I really care about you, but by talking so much with you there I'm missing out on life here." Once we went on the one-communication-a-week plan, my European contacts blossomed.

When Europe Was the Cure for a Big Breakup

The next time you go through a big breakup, don't go for psychiatrists, meds, or manicures—book a European vacay. I learned the wonders of this remedy on my third visit. My friend and I had just gotten out of serious relationships that weren't right for various reasons. We were more than ready for major *fiesta*-ing. We tried out every restaurant, club, pub, banquet, and plaza party. We channeled the sexiest dance moves and experimented with an assortment of sassy fashions. It was amazingly adventurous. What we learned: three dates a day is ideal . . . one for breakfast, lunch, and dinner. OK, so I only hit that jackpot once, but it was so therapeutic. In no time, when asked if we missed our ex-boyfriends, we responded, "What ex-boyfriends?" Europe is most definitely the single girl's dream.

When Miss Beautiful Regretted
Clinging to a Bad Boyfriend

If you are currently in a wonderful relationship, don't end it just for your trip. Most ladies only get one chance at Prince Charming. But if you have already kissed the right toad, you probably aren't reading this book. On the other hand, if you are in a relationship that clearly isn't right, fearlessly break it off before flying across the ocean. One of my girlfriends didn't and learned the hard way that this was a mistake. She was beyond beautiful with an incredible sense of humor, but her boyfriend did not appreciate his treasure. She kept trying to make their relationship work. When she went abroad, she faithfully stayed in contact with him and turned down all European invites. Her welcome home gift: finding her BF in the arms of a GF. My girlfriend felt like she not only lost her companion and her girlfriend, but the best part of her European trip. She doesn't know when, if ever, she will get the opportunity to go abroad again. Bad boyfriends are never worth passing up European princes.

Tip #12:
Don't Hide Out—You're in Europe!

You might be thinking, "Who does she think I am? Like I'm going to come all the way to Europe and hide out! I'll skip this tip. It doesn't apply to me." *Pleeeaaase* keep reading. Even the savviest socialites find themselves trapped in towns suffering from masculine droughts. Then they typically quit trying to meet European men and miss out on the best part of the trip when they could easily change the scenery instead. Just as some land is more fertile than others, some male hunting grounds are more fertile than others.

When the European It Girl Was Not It

I witnessed a great example of anti-hiding-out when I went on one European trip with my hilarious girlfriend. She was inundated with men—emphasis on the "date" in "inundated." Every time I got asked out on one date, Miss Popular got asked out on two. I simply couldn't keep up. She had the draw of Poison Ivy except that she didn't have a drop of evil blood. When she looked at him, no native knight-in-shining-armor could break his gaze with her big brown eyes. Men were equally drawn to her funny and charming personality. She could keep anyone laughing. But I don't care how strong your talents are at joke-telling, if there are no guys to listen, no guys will laugh. The following summer, Miss Popular returned to Europe to study. She picked a location that was full of education, history, and beautiful landscapes but void of male-meeting hot spots. In this serene town, eligible men were almost an extinct species. She solved this problem by traveling to lively locations on weekends and regained her title of "European It Girl."

Pre-planning so you can hit the hot spots is the cardinal rule for encountering eligible European men—and I don't just mean heading out to the favorites listed in this guide. Although my girlfriends and I found ultra-success while visiting them, Europe is constantly creating new manmarks. Asking prospective guys around town what new happening hot spots have opened is an easy, nonthreatening way to meet them. So regardless of where your European trip takes you, don't hide out. There are always options for meeting European men and having a great time.

Tip #13:
Avoid Prowling in Packs

Imagine you're walking into a room filled with strangers. Are you more likely to approach one cutie immersed in a herd of friends or another casually chatting with a sidekick? The twosome is so much easier to attempt. Most men don't want to tackle a gang of girls to reach their prime prospect. Europeans are no different. Ladies, I know you are hungry for grade-A males, but don't act like wolves on the hunt—traveling in a pack is the wrong approach.

When My Fiery Friend and I Left the Pack

Many girls like to plan big group outings. Once when I studied abroad with twenty other females, one of them nominated herself Social Chair. Every night she mapped out our schedule of where to meet, what restaurant to dine at, and the bar or show with which to wrap up our evening. Evites were distributed and everyone was expected to blindly follow. At first I joined in. Despite the fact that all these girls wanted to meet guys, this plan was not designed for romance. Of course, no European men approached any of us in this flock of females. After a couple of days, my very fiery friend and I refused to follow the itinerary. We grabbed a third girly and formed our own plans. Our top priority was meeting European males. With this small group we each succeeded on our first attempt . . . and every time after that.

The other seventeen gals pressured us to stay in the clan. We didn't buckle, but they continued to give us grief and we heard whispered comments like, "How can they possibly be having fun?" They saw how when different European Jacks arrived night after night to escort us to dinner and dancing. Then they started traveling in smaller groups too, with similar results. They quickly transformed from Followers to European Male Finds!

Tip #14:
Don't Cling to Men
from Your Own Country

Travelers seem to have a tendency to stick with those from their own country. The way they interact with foreigners is kind of like the way boys and girls interacted when we had dances in middle school. The boys gathered on one side of the room and the girls on the other. Friends, we're no longer in middle school! It's time to mingle. Quit hanging out in your comfort zone next to the guys from home. A European wonder usually won't risk going through your gatekeepers to show you a fabulous time. Muster the courage to venture into the native-male territory. You will like what you find.

Another common observation is that when single men and women travel abroad in a group, they quickly pair up. We all have plenty of opportunities to date local men when we return home, but how many chances do we have to experience European men in their native habitat? Don't let a man from your own country monopolize you—unless he is so special that you want to keep him when you return. Going on dates with European wowers is an adventure not to be missed without an extremely good reason. There is a sort of wonder involved when two people come together who are from different parts of the world. It is hard to describe, kind of like trying to explain how chocolate tastes to someone who has never experienced it. Like chocolate, you will definitely want to experience European men again and again.

It is also important to never toy with the emotions of guys from your own country—or of any men for that matter. Because I have a brother, I feel very strongly about this. Guys often act tough, but they can still get their feelings hurt. While you are in Europe, letting the males from your country know up front that you want to get to know the locals is really the best way to go. Then they shouldn't feel bad if you don't respond to their advances. I know several girls who each clung to an M.O.S. (Member of the Opposite Sex) from their own country until they got the courage to meet enticing Europeans. Then they abandoned their hometowners. This not only caused the homeboys unhappiness, but made the European prospects think that they weren't nice.

When Bar Wrecker's Boyfriend Was Thrown Behind Bars

I have a girlfriend—let's call her Bar Wrecker—who would never intentionally hurt anyone. Last summer she had the opportunity to study in Denmark for five weeks. Being in a foreign country and knowing no natives, she unfortunately fell into the trap of clinging to a guy in the group from her home university. Bar Wrecker was not interested in her Hometown Honey as a long-term prospect, but for the first four and a half weeks they were inseparable. In his mind, they were a couple. In hers, they were just having summer fun. On the last weekend of her stay, my girlfriend started having serious European man remorse. She had been in Denmark for almost five weeks and had only seen the backs of the Danish men's heads. This was because they passed her by while she clung to her hometown escort. During her last night out on the town, Bar Wrecker and Hometown Honey went to Copenhagen's famous festival, Midsummer Night's Eve. The beach was swarming with dashing Danes. The desire to meet one of them became so strong that my friend desperately tried to escape her American man, even though they had come together.

Bar Wrecker succeeded at slipping away from Hometown Honey for a brief moment when a Danish army officer introduced himself to her. He was so charming that she was ready to march in line with his rank. Overtaken with his exotic aura and not thinking about Hometown Honey, she pretended that she had nothing to do with her domestic lover and joined Officer D for drinks at a beach bar. Nothing to do with him? Had she been hypnotized for the past several weeks while she was dating him nonstop? Well, the "non" part of nonstop turned into nonexistent—what she hoped Hometown Honey would become. Her companion was left abandoned at a festival among strangers. Furious, he followed Bar Wrecker and Officer D to the bar. Hometown Honey sat at another table glaring at the girl he considered his girlfriend. He proceeded to have eight too many beers. All the while, Officer D was getting pretty concerned about my friend's "stalker." Hometown Honey got so drunk and angry that he slammed his fist down on the table, toppling an ornate cut-glass lamp, which crashed to the floor, sending shattered pieces everywhere. The police were called and he got to spend his last weekend abroad in a Danish jail.

My friend realized too late that she should have mustered the courage to date the Danes instead of clinging to Hometown Honey. She felt really bad for leading him on, and sadly cut short her evening with Officer D to try to help him get out of jail. Copenhagen has many attractions, but Bar Wrecker can attest that the House of Corrections is not a man-meeting hot spot. She offered all the money she had to the officers of the law for bail, but it wasn't enough. With no other options, she called Hometown Honey's parents and asked them to wire the money. Unfortunately, it didn't get there in time for him to miss out on a slumber party behind bars—and there was no sleeping for him that night.

My girlfriend learned three important lessons from her Danish fiasco: when in Europe, don't cling to men from home; never lead a guy on if you aren't interested in him; and realize that Danish men are gentlemen. Even after Officer D caught on to the fact that Bar

Wrecker had been dating Hometown Honey and politely rescinded his offer to entertain her that evening, he paid for her cab home. Too bad she didn't dare to date the Danes earlier.

 MAN-MEETING TIDBIT. If you are traveling with a guy friend, you definitely don't have to exclude him to meet native men. On one of my European trips, I had a close male friend in my group. He was very nice, had a sister he had grown up protecting, and refused to let me and my girlfriend hit the town alone, even though we were in a safe area. Of course, in this scenario we were happy to have him along. He turned into a European man-meeting asset. We helped him find women while he helped us meet men—and the guys seemed to realize that if any one of them treated us less than par he would never forget it once my friend's brotherly instincts took over. So no matter what situation you are in, you can enjoy the European guys and still stay on great terms with the men from your own country.

Tip #15:
You're Never a Loser When You're Alone

Have you ever wanted to go out but your BFF's were being boring—aka just wanted to sit on their butts, eat potato chips, and stare at the TV? This may seem unlikely when they are visiting Europe, but it happens. Not just once but several times when I was traveling, my girlfriends and I had exciting plans. Then at the last minute they got mesmerized by the tube and never made it off the couch.

Refuse to let duddy traveling companions ruin your fun. Realize that part of their problem is fear. It is much easier for them to live vicariously through someone else's experiences on a TV show than to create their own excitement. Don't let them drag you into this trap! Go it alone if you must—that is, during the day when it is safe to fly solo. Snack at a charming coffee shop, visit the hippest shopping center, or relax at a beautiful beach. Tell your friends how much fun it is in the outside world. Then when the sun sets and you should not venture out alone, pull the gals away from the plasmas and force them to face the town.

When Flying Solo Landed a Dinner Date

My friend first put this rule to the test while studying in France. Midterms were approaching and she was swamped with work. All of her classmates became hermits and locked themselves in the library— totally uneventful! If you can pick up a guy in there, then kudos to you. The most I ever picked up at the library was a free pair of earplugs. This *ambitieux* attracter took her textbooks to a cozy little café instead. Just thirty minutes after she had started sipping a beverage and memorizing flash cards, the waiter approached her. He pointed at an attractive Frenchman sitting alone and explained, "That *homme à femmes* requests your company for dinner." To sum it up, dinner was just the appetizer to their relationship. Don't ask how her grades turned out, but rest assured that her love life thrived. You know the college motto "You can retake a class but not a weekend." It's even truer on a European trip.

When a European Song Was Dedicated to Me

The next time I returned to Europe, I followed my girlfriend's lead. The day I really hit the solo jackpot was when I went to London. I wanted to brunch at this restaurant that was located in the middle of the arts district and shaped like a miniature theater, complete with a stage where famous opera singers performed. Patrons dined at tables in the balcony, boxes, and orchestra pit. I knew that this was an opportunity not to be missed, but oddly enough none of my friends were interested. I didn't let this stop me. I made a reservation for one, got all done-up, and headed out.

The host seated me at the only table onstage, next to the pianist. The lead singer dedicated a song to me while the waiter served me what seemed like ten courses. By the sixth scrumptious course, I was completely in heaven and totally stuffed. My waiter thought that I had stopped eating because I was unsatisfied with my roast and brought me a complimentary chocolate mousse cake. Somehow whenever it comes to dessert, more room opens up. After my meal, a bundle of blokes asked me to join their table for tea. They gave me the lowdown on that week's hot happenings around town and invited me to come along. I'm so glad that I dared to do in this place alone.

Tip #16:
Use Getting Lost to Your Advantage

Do you suffer from directional dyslexia? If so, turn this weakness into a man-meeting strength. When you are lost in Europe don't ask the kind elderly lady or police officer for help—that is, unless the latter is single and has a great personality. Instead, approach the most appealing male native. European gentlemen are usually happy to help a damsel in distress. Getting lost is a great excuse to grab their attention. And if your case of directional dyslexia is as severe as mine, you will get top opportunities practically every day. I have probably met 40 percent of my foreign prospects this way.

When My Directional Dyslexia Led Me
to Lust-Worthy Males

One evening my girlfriend and I put lost time to good male use as we prepared to meet two guys for a double date. They had asked us out and made all the necessary arrangements the previous day, just as we arrived in the city. Of course, we played it safe and arranged to meet our two new European cuties at a restaurant instead of letting them pick us up. There was just one problem with that plan. Although the gents had given us detailed instructions on where and when to meet them, at the time, we knew almost nothing about our surroundings.

The next night when we left for this liaison, our directional dyslexia was seriously acting up. First, we got on the right metro going the wrong way. Next, we landed on the wrong metro altogether. We got off at a beach where tons of townspeople were partying by bonfires. That would have been wonderful if we were supposed to meet there, but we weren't. We were disoriented, but not enough to miss two other male European treats who barely spoke our language—and we definitely didn't speak theirs. We asked them for help, but their directions made no sense. After several attempts, they finally formed words we understood, "Join us for big fire on beach where cook food. Romantic. No?" We tried to explain that we had agreed to join some other guys. They pointed to themselves and said, "More handsome than other guys you meet!" We came to a meeting of the minds. They helped us find our destination and we agreed to get together with them for lunch the following day.

Caveat. Clearly, getting lost is a great mechanism for meeting sizzling sights of the opposite sex. But bear in mind that if you are lost and sense danger, a police officer is the ideal person to ask for help, even if he does not have rendezvous-potential or if he is wearing a wedding ring. My girlfriends and I were always safe. We researched all the areas where we went in advance, never meant to get lost, always made a point of arranging to meet up with new prospects in public, and did not stay with anyone or in any place that made us feel uneasy. Even so, when I was on my way to the Formula 1 race, I accidentally made a wrong turn into a sketchy neighborhood. You bet I asked the two cops each carrying eight guns for help! So just use good judgment and always have a cell phone on hand with your host country's emergency numbers programmed in it. I always did this and never had to use them, but you cannot make yourself too safe.

How to Act

Just as you should not clap in the middle of an oration or drink before a toast, you should not break the European man-meeting code of conduct if you want successful foreign encounters. Here are the key elements.

Tip #17:
Be Inviting, Not Overbearing

The native male thoroughbreds typically track down bewitching beauties and run from barracudas. Now, when I say "beauties," you must understand that in Europe you honestly don't have to be the stereotypical long-legged, big-boobed Barbie look-alike to attract the guys. In this region, a girl's beauty is not generally classified by a certain look but by how she plays up what she has—and the persona she puts forth. Every female has something spectacular to offer. If she accentuates it, she can be perceived as a total bird!

When the Girl Next Door Got All the Gorgeous Guys

One of my best friends is not what most men would typically call attractive. Around her US university she was considered one of the guys, not one to ask out. I sadly heard some frat boys refer to her as homely. But in Europe she was a sex siren. Honestly, the gents who asked her out had bodies that put *Men's Fitness* models to shame. They were intelligent and accomplished, and each was a wonderful conversationalist. Best of all, they adored my friend even though she was nowhere near model-thin and joked that she had hips made for childbearing.

This European male magnet was an expert at using her assets. Her shiny black hair was breathtaking. She always wore it down and frequently ran her fingers through the tendrils to attract stares. Of course it worked! And it obviously didn't hurt that she put forth 110 percent effort into being bewitching. She was very inviting without throwing herself at the men. She would say "hi" in a playful tone, ask a legit question about directions or where to eat lunch, or casually comment on the beautiful view and then slowly walk away. As she did, she would look at the men out of the corners of her eyes, as if to say, "You know you like me." She often glanced back and always gave them time to come up with an excuse to intersect her path. Naturally, she would also turn her head, tossing that showstopping hair.

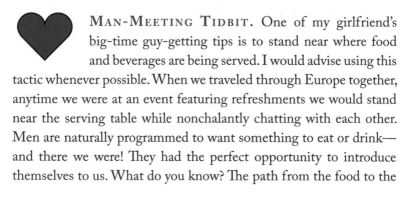 MAN-MEETING TIDBIT. One of my girlfriend's big-time guy-getting tips is to stand near where food and beverages are being served. I would advise using this tactic whenever possible. When we traveled through Europe together, anytime we were at an event featuring refreshments we would stand near the serving table while nonchalantly chatting with each other. Men are naturally programmed to want something to eat or drink—and there we were! They had the perfect opportunity to introduce themselves to us. What do you know? The path from the food to the

men's restroom is also an optimum place for date-trolling. So follow my shiny-haired friend's example. She is the prototype for how to get these local lovers to love you. Her success rate was 89 percent.

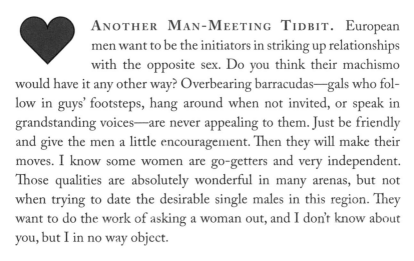 ANOTHER MAN-MEETING TIDBIT. European men want to be the initiators in striking up relationships with the opposite sex. Do you think their machismo would have it any other way? Overbearing barracudas—gals who follow in guys' footsteps, hang around when not invited, or speak in grandstanding voices—are never appealing to them. Just be friendly and give the men a little encouragement. Then they will make their moves. I know some women are go-getters and very independent. Those qualities are absolutely wonderful in many arenas, but not when trying to date the desirable single males in this region. They want to do the work of asking a woman out, and I don't know about you, but I in no way object.

Tip #18:
Be Upbeat

European gentlemen are drawn to ladies who smile, laugh, and aren't uptight. They carefully note any change in your mood and are particularly concerned if you become upset.

When a Smile Was My Best Accessory

I first learned that men are drawn to upbeat girls one night while dancing with a suave Scot. I noticed that my girlfriend was missing. She was nervous and had agreed to tell me if she decided to step out of the room for any reason. I became worried as I scanned the dance floor and didn't see her. The Scot, not realizing what had happened, commented, "You were so fun a second ago. Why suddenly so serious?" As I left him in search of my friend, other local males approached me and voiced similar concerns, explaining that they had watched me dancing and observed the change in my demeanor. From this and other experiences, I found that foreign guys are aware of our moods. They are happiest with happy girls.

When a Tan Italian Came to My Rescue at 4 AM

If you truly have a problem, most European men will gladly do whatever it takes to come to your rescue as long as they have gotten to know your cute personality and don't think you're just being a drama queen. Many times they saved my friends and me in tough situations. One example occurred after I danced the night away with a tan Italian named Enrique. This was in one of those European cities where the nightlife starts after midnight and ends when the sun rises. By 4 AM, although the club was hopping, I knew that I should be getting home. I had finals the following week and needed to get some sleep and start studying, but my girlfriends did not want to leave. Enrique said it was unsafe for me to hail a cab by myself, so he gave up his club pass to escort me outside. We knew that the area was known for hosting impromptu festivals, but since the club did not have windows and the music was loud, we didn't realize that a celebration was in full swing outside. We found the sidewalks and streets crowded with literally thousands of happily inebriated, face-painted revelers shouting, shoving, and singing—but not a single available taxi. Because of the crowds, none of them could make it into the area.

My Italian escort and I attempted to return to the club; however, the festival was moving in the opposite direction, which made that impossible. In fact, the streets were so congested and the partiers so numerous that drivers had difficulty getting through the intersections. *L'Italiano* grabbed my hand to keep from losing me. While we wove through the congestion in search of a cab, a policeman approached us, complimented my new friend for his chivalry, and confided that I was fortunate to have my "boyfriend" watching over me.

My protector's apartment was nearby. He suggested that we walk there so I could get some sleep until the crowds died down. He promised to take me home in the morning so I could start studying. I explained that I didn't feel comfortable with this plan since we had only just met. He said that he understood and would make sure I got home safely. After an hour and a half, we finally passed through the heart of the festival and found a cab zone. It had an inordinately long line, but no cabs. Like most European guys who have gotten to know a girl and realized that she is in serious need, my new Italian was more than willing to keep helping me. He spent another hour getting me safely home, and it didn't end with that. For the rest of my stay he continued to ask me out and even invited me to be his guest in Verona.

Tip #19:
Break Through Language Barriers

If you're visiting a country with a language that you don't know, give it a go. Most men don't care if you're not fluent; they just want you to make an attempt. While on your trip, turn on the TV and pick up a few phrases. Then throw them around whenever possible. This, combined with pantomiming, will successfully get you through almost any encounter.

When I Learned the International
Language of Pantomime

One night in Europe, I met this Swedish stud who did not speak English. My knowledge of his language was limited to *hej* and *ja*. His knowledge of my language was limited to "My name is Sven." That plus pantomiming was enough for us to have fun the entire evening. Sven introduced himself and then asked me to dance by motioning with his hands. I said "ja" and we went on from there. After that we seriously relied on acting. It was actually quite funny. When in doubt, laugh. That is the natural thing to do in this situation. If you can laugh at yourself, all usually goes well.

From Sven, I learned some pantomiming lingo. If a man holds up his hand like he is drinking from an imaginary glass and then points at you, that means, "I'm going to take a break and get a drink. Would you like one?" When a guy fans himself, points at the door, and then motions for you to follow, that means, "It's ridiculously hot in here. Would you like to step out on the terrace with me for some fresh air?" When a man takes your hand, leads you to the dance floor, and then points at your girlfriend and nods at his guy friend, that means, "Let's dance—and buddy [addressing his guy friend], get your butt on the dance floor, because there is a desirable available partner." And if a guy strokes your hair, that means, "I want to kiss you. If you don't give me the OK signal right away, I'm going to try anyway . . . because, hey, we're in Europe!" As you can see, pantomiming is a rare case in which pointing is entirely appropriate. So don't let your lack of fluidity in a foreign language stop you from having a great vacation. Get down a couple of phrases and pantomime.

When Trying to Speak Spanish Scored Points

When I traveled to Spain for the second time, I first realized that what counts is not how well a single girl knows the local language, but how willing she is to try to learn it. I went on a date with a Barcelonan businessman. By then, I could converse in Spanish, but my pronunciation was horrendous. I was the Eliza Doolittle of España. My date worked for a Latin company with a branch in the United States, and he spoke Spanish and English perfectly. I was embarrassed about my lack of mastery of the Spanish language, but he warmly encouraged me to speak his native tongue. He explained that he liked my accent and just wanted me to try. Whenever I did, he conversed with me in Spanish and acted as though he was charmed by my attempt. With his encouragement, my Spanish improved more in one evening than in a month of Spanish classes. My knowledge of Spanish became good enough to allow me to have extended relationships with Spaniards. This was definitely not the case on my first trip to Spain, when I had my car race fiasco.

When Pantomiming Lasted for Five Dates

If you really do not know the language and you meet an enticing man who cannot speak yours, the relationship will not go far unless you start taking language classes. Another girlfriend of mine spent a month in Denmark. While she was out one night at Rust, a swanky club, she met an attractive Dane. Attractiveness was the attribute she was drawn to since he hardly spoke English and she knew absolutely no Danish. They went on five dates—which is an incredible amount when verbal contact is at a minimum. She said after that it just got too hard to communicate, so she moved on to men who knew more of her language.

Luckily, quite a few Europeans do speak multiple languages, but please give their native tongues a whirl even if you fail miserably. They will appreciate it, and most of them will reward you with a wonderful time.

Tip #20:
Catch Up on Current Events

My very studious girlfriend didn't discriminate. She studied men just as much as neuroscience. Her favorite *Homo sapiens*? Easy answer—European males! She was quite well traveled, multilingual, and able to wrap any European chap right around her little finger. Her secret was to research local events and use them to her advantage.

From watching her work, I noticed that many European guys take more pride in their land of inheritance than in their own names.

Before this sexy scholar traveled to a new city, she read books, articles, and blogs about it. While in the town, she scanned the local newspaper daily. She got a thorough overview, from historical perspectives and political facts to fashion forecasts.

When Miss Smarty Snatched a SAM (Sought After Man)

A typical example of how Miss Smarty used her gray matter to snatch a SAM happened while she was lunching at a chic café. A particularly enticing highbrow was reading his newspaper at the next table. She noticed him lingering on a certain article. What do you know? She had read the exact one earlier that morning. She cleverly stopped to ask him the location of the nearest restroom. Then, pretending like she just noticed his article, she casually dropped a pithy comment concerning the controversy. He looked impressed and asked if she had moved to the area. Her response: "I'm just visiting, but I'm into learning the European culture." She proceeded to ask an intelligent question. Sold! Her admirer responded, "I have to leave now for a meeting and that question has no easy answer. Let's discuss it over dinner." Bingo! She was en route to a jealousy-evoking date in the ultra-ritzy region.

Don't think you have to be in Albert Einstein's gene pool to impress gents with your local knowledge. If you are fluent enough to read the paper, can you memorize a few pivotal points and show that you are all about the new land? Of course you can.

Tip #21:
Be Fast to Allure and Slow to Succumb

How you use this tip is dependent upon your desired outcome. If you want to have a romantic European evening, be wined and dined, and get asked out again and again, be fast to allure and slow to succumb to the men's sexual advances. On the other hand, if you are just into random play or have a hookup map to fill like my friend the Sexcapader, then you should still be fast to allure but the "slow to succumb" part of this tip does not apply to your vacation plan.

Out of the myriad girls I know who have been to Europe, none of the ones who slept with a native guy on the night they met got asked out, only one got asked out again after having sex with a man on their first date, and only two after having sex on the second date. The rest had to be slower to succumb to sexual advances in order to be treated well and continue the courtship. Actually, many said that when they moved too fast, the men turned mean.

Some females from certain regions have the reputation among European males as being sexually loose and many men are happy to accommodate them. So if you are a Sexcapader, no matter where you are from, getting stars on your map should be a cinch. In fact, my friend who created her erotic memoirs said that sometimes she went after guys who didn't speak her language because communication got in the way of her goal. She did say, though, that she was really glad she took the time to put away her hookup map and have her one European relationship—the Berlin student who hitchhiked to visit her in France. She confided that this was the only guy she really got to know before becoming intimate. He treated her like a "queen." To this day, she still talks about how she wishes more men were that romantic.

When the Man-whore Became a Gentleman

A typical example of this principle in practice occurred the evening that I met Joaquín, my curly-haired Casanova. I wanted to be asked out on dates, treated well, and be asked out again. Joaquín introduced himself while my friend and I were entering the club, and instantly invited me to come home with him. Don't be thrown if a European man asks you to spend the night within the first minutes of meeting—it doesn't mean you look like a hooker. In many instances, European men are more sexually open than men from other areas. Understanding this, I politely declined, saying that I didn't know him.

The Spanish *hombre de negocios* replied, "No problem. Let's get to know each other now." FYI, "getting to know each other" can be code for exchanging lots of saliva. I explained that I still didn't know him well enough to "get to know" him. This tipped the scale and he asked, "How about a date tomorrow? The movies?" When I took a second to respond, he went on, "Maybe you're not the movie kind of girl. How about a fancy restaurant? I'll take you anywhere you want." From then on, he was a total gentleman and lots of fun.

That same night, my stunning girlfriend began making out within fifteen minutes of meeting a mint. She was shocked when he didn't even ask for her number and left to "get to know" another girl. It didn't matter that she had the most flawless figure in the club. She was left dateless the next day. Once she learned that European hot cats live for the chase, she had them waiting in line to ask her out.

When Miss In-the-Moment Got the DO-YA
(*Dropped On Your Ass*)

My other girlfriend, let's call her Miss In-the-Moment, was not normally into random play, but one night in Europe she decided to make an exception. She met this native guy in a ritzy lounge. He said he was a professional athlete and he had these beautiful kiteboarding biceps. He bought her drinks and they got along great. He acted completely into her. After about twenty minutes, they decided to leave the lounge to talk outside on a bench with a romantic view. Well, they didn't really talk . . . they made out the whole time. After an hour, Mr. Fast Mover convinced Miss In-the-Moment to let him come to her apartment. Then he convinced her to let him spend the night. She reasoned that they had only known each other for less than an hour and a half, but it was the *best* less than an hour and a half of her trip! And he was definitely falling for her! *Or, definitely maybe not?*

In the morning, she went to school while he stayed sprawled out in her bed. Still in euphoria over his good looks and the warm feeling of his beautiful biceps, my friend asked for his number. Don't get too excited. There is not a happy ending to this story. Mr. Fast Mover, now Mr. Lazy Head, said he didn't have a phone. An email address? *Nope.* How about a street address? *In the process of moving.* To where, a cave? So this man didn't have any appliances of the new millennium yet he was in touch enough to attend the ritziest lounge in the area and could afford to buy my friend drinks the night before? More like he had gotten all he wanted out of her on the first evening and felt like there was no chase. He did set up a place to meet her later that day. You might think I'm being hard on him—keep reading. *He NEVER showed.* Hard on him? Not even close. All he wanted was some ass. Then my friend got the DO-YA—pronounced like "Do ya?" As in, "Do ya wannna be dropped on your ass?" *I don't think so!* This girl and every member of the SGA (<u>S</u>ingle <u>G</u>irls' <u>A</u>ssociation) deserve so much more than that.

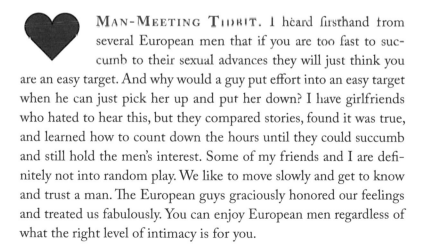

MAN-MEETING TIDBIT. I heard firsthand from several European men that if you are too fast to succumb to their sexual advances they will just think you are an easy target. And why would a guy put effort into an easy target when he can just pick her up and put her down? I have girlfriends who hated to hear this, but they compared stories, found it was true, and learned how to count down the hours until they could succumb and still hold the men's interest. Some of my friends and I are definitely not into random play. We like to move slowly and get to know and trust a man. The European guys graciously honored our feelings and treated us fabulously. You can enjoy European men regardless of what the right level of intimacy is for you.

Tip #22:
Don't Give Up

No matter how much glam you have going for you, how high your charm meter registers, or how faithfully you are following these tips, there will always be certain bozos who pass you by. Some might even be rude in the process. All nationalities have chaps with chips on their shoulders. Don't be discouraged. Forget about those no-goes. Move on. The next one could be a winner.

When Miss Porcelain Was Rejected and Then Regaled

I witnessed this scenario at a European club with my stunning girl-friend. She had pale blue eyes, natural blonde hair that was so light it was almost white, and porcelain skin. We were surrounded by Latin Antonio Banderas look-alikes. She was definitely the draw. While dancing with a dashing man, she glanced at her phone to check the time. Seeing this, he sarcastically presumed in a very loud voice, "I bet you want my number. Every girl does. I'm not interested." Over-hearing this remark, another guy blurted out, "Good, because there's no room in her phone for egomaniacs!" Ten minutes later, the most drop-dead gorgeous man approached my girlfriend. They danced the night away while the narcissist stood alone, sulking. Was he in high demand? No way.

There are so many European male possibilities. Don't get hung up on that rotten egg who rejects you.

Tip #23:
Saying Goodnight

If you have met an over-the-top enticing European man, don't think that saying goodnight means you will never see him again. Leaving while he still wants more will increase your odds of being asked out. But never just say that you have to leave without giving an adequate reason, because your new love interest will believe you are not enjoying his company. "I'm tired" is not a good option. He will think you mean that you're tired of him. Having to get up early for an important appointment is an appropriate excuse, as long as you express what a great time you had with him and that you are sad to leave so soon. This will open the door for him to ask, "What's your phone number? I want to see you again." Always make an encouraging response, such as "Me too!" Then the deal is done—you're on for the date!

When I Won and Lost Oskar in One Night

Sadly, I learned this tip the hard way. I was at a sophisticated European club and met this beyond-amazing local guy named Oskar. We really got along. He was everything that a girl would want—smart, funny, attentive, handsome, successful . . . you get the visual.

Well, the evening we met, I started coming down with a miserable cold. It was one of those nasty bugs where you feel great leaving for the evening and then *wham*, your head starts pounding and you feel like you have been run over by a Mack truck. Unfortunately, the Mack truck sensation came when Oskar and I were dancing in the loudest section of the club. It was kind of hard to hear each other and Oskar thought that I had gotten quiet all of a sudden because I was tired of talking over the noise. Instead, I wasn't exactly feeling my riproaring best. Oskar suggested that we go upstairs to a beautiful indoor courtyard for drinks by the waterfall where we could hear each other better. I really wanted to go, but cold doldrums were seriously stopping me. I explained that I was exhausted and should be getting home to bed.

Oskar looked hurt and replied, "You could have just told me you weren't interested." With my pounding head and the pulsating music, I couldn't think of a comeback before he disappeared. My concerned girlfriend approached and commented, "He really liked you and treated you nicer than I have ever seen any guy treat any girl." When I explained what had happened, she said, "If only you had told him that you weren't feeling well and that you would really like to see him again, he would have definitely taken you out another night."

I regretted not responding better to Oskar. I can only imagine what I missed out on. When I was over my cold, I went back to the club with the hope of seeing him again, but he wasn't there. Shout out to Oskar, if you are reading this . . . which I highly doubt because you aren't a single girl . . . but if you ever hear about this and see me again in Europe, please give me another chance!

Luckily, you members of the SGA can learn from my mistakes and not miss out on the Oskars of Europe by knowing how to say goodnight.

How to Score in Outdoor Adventures

You adrenaline junkies may like the thought of spontaneously snatching endorphins, skiing down the slopes as fast as possible, running the track at record-breaking speeds, and cycling ahead of the champs, but slow down for a moment to read what will make you win the man-meeting race. Many of the tips below can be used in everyday European guy-getting endeavors, but are especially powerful in outdoor activities. So, just as you may not want to hike only five miles when you can do ten, when it comes to meeting European men, you may not want to stop at a few hot dates when you can have several.

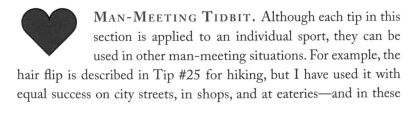 MAN-MEETING TIDBIT. Although each tip in this section is applied to an individual sport, they can be used in other man-meeting situations. For example, the hair flip is described in Tip #25 for hiking, but I have used it with equal success on city streets, in shops, and at eateries—and in these

venues a girl doesn't have to worry about getting hot if she wears her hair down.

Tip #24:
Use Chairlifts to Your Advantage

Being able to navigate the slopes is important for having skiing flings with Alps men. But in order to meet them you must first know how to navigate the chairlift. Many look at this as merely a mode of transportation, but my girlfriends have used it as a mode of meeting European men. So don't be too eager to jump into that chairlift line. Stand back and people-watch. See what appealing guys are coming and when. Then you can hit the slopes with a hot prospect.

Most guys don't go skiing with an exactly even-numbered group, meaning one of them will have to ride in the chair with a stranger. You want that one to be a charming stunner and for you to be the stranger. Once you are all alone on the lift with that appealing skier, he will have no one to talk with but you. So wait until that special someone gets in line and go in after him. If you two hit it off, he will not want to leave you when the ride is over. This is the perfect opportunity for him to ask if you would like to ski down the slope with him. Of course your answer will be "yes." And when he asks if you want to enjoy dinner that evening, your answer will be "yes" again. And when he asks if you want to meet up the next day, well you know what your answer will be. But what you don't know is how your relationship will end . . . that is, if it does.

There is something aphrodisiac-esque about the snow. I have a friend who met her European boyfriend skiing and after two years they are still dating. She was just offered a job in Switzerland. Now they can be together all the time. Who knows, the love bug might bite you too! Or you may not be in the mood for a serious relationship and just want to find a wower to share an outing with. Either way, the chairlift is where it's at.

Tip #25:
Male Hikers Cannot Resist the Hair Flip

Just hiking will not normally give you an in with European men. It's hiking with flair that ignites the spark for an introduction. The hair flip is like cupid's arrow. Without it, your target may not be struck with love-itis. When fixing your hair the morning of a hike, it's vital that you not pull it all up in a sports bun. I know it feels unbearable to wear your hair all the way down while working out in the heat, so try either pulling part of it back or putting it all in a ponytail. Just make sure that enough hair is loose for adequate flipage.

Once you are on the trail, check out the beautiful scenery and the men in your vicinity. If you see a husky hunk, glance at him, smile, and continue walking. Wait one second and flip your hair. This can either be done by flicking your hair out with your hand or shaking your head. Then allow your hiker to hunt you down. It shouldn't take him any time to catch up with you. Generally in European cultures, once a girl has given a guy the clue that she could be interested, if he is attracted to her, he will close in. What I enjoy most about these natives is their ability to be uninhibited. They go straight for the gold. Let them notice the gold in you by flirtatiously flipping your hair.

Tip #26:
Avoid the Bubble Butt

Many of my chums who are heavily involved in butt-intensive activities like skating, hiking, biking, and climbing have muscles of steel. That's awesome until you start bulking up so much that instead of having a firm, hot hiney, you have a full-blown bubble butt. In sports like biking and climbing, where it is critical to wear tight clothing and you spend most of the time with your bootie stuck up in the air for every guy to examine, it's imperative that you show off a bodacious derrière. If you have a bubble butt, there is hope. Pilates is out there. It is a form of exercise that elongates muscles and leaves bodies strong and elegant. You can either hire an instructor for individual or small-group lessons where you use specially constructed machines, or you can take larger mat classes concentrating on floor exercises.

When a Bubble Butt Became a Bodacious Derrière

One of my gal pals is a competitive figure skater. She works out about eight hours a day, and she is very beguiling but so strong that she could take out almost any male. Unfortunately, about a year ago she developed the dreaded bubble butt and man thighs. She was beyond self-conscious. She even stopped wearing shorts, and when she and some friends took a trip to Europe, she refused to come climbing. After returning home, she decided that was no way to live life. She enrolled in Pilates and soon started seeing results. Her muscles were so bulky that perfection took four months, but now she has an enviable rear end. She could throw on the lingerie and angel wings and double for Alessandra Ambrosio on the runway.

For anyone interested in butt-building sports, Pilates is a good bubble-butt antidote. Actually, Pilates is an excellent idea for anyone who wants to look as good going as she does coming.

How to Be
the Light of Nightlife

Listen up, ladies who love nightlife. This is the deal make-or-break section in the guy-getting department for all of you, from those who just want to relax in a lounge with a drink and a fascinating European man by their side to the dancing darlings who want to jive for hours on end.

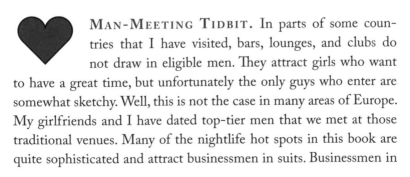 MAN-MEETING TIDBIT. In parts of some countries that I have visited, bars, lounges, and clubs do not draw in eligible men. They attract girls who want to have a great time, but unfortunately the only guys who enter are somewhat sketchy. Well, this is not the case in many areas of Europe. My girlfriends and I have dated top-tier men that we met at those traditional venues. Many of the nightlife hot spots in this book are quite sophisticated and attract businessmen in suits. Businessmen in

suits at clubs? You know it! And not just any old clubs—ones with chandeliers, marble floors, and etched staircases.

Of course, Europe has some seedy shacks like anyplace else, but the hot spots in this guide will clue you in on many of the highs so you can skip the lows. Since the highs are so heavenly, it is important to know how to be the light of nightlife.

Tip #27:
Pause When Ordering a Drink

European guys look for opportunities to suavely meet girls. There are only so many ways they can charmingly approach a lady, so make it easy on them. When ordering a drink at a bar, in a lounge, or while clubbing, pause for a moment when deciding what you want. This gives prospects a chance to notice you, approach, and offer to buy your drink. In no way are you acting like a gold digger by doing this. Many European men love to treat women to beverages. It is an easy method for them to make an introduction. What should you give Mr. Drink Buyer in return? Only a short, polite conversation or a dance is needed. Some girls might think they owe him nothing. I say, "Not true." Besides the fact that it is inconsiderate, men don't appreciate being treated like human ready-teller machines. The goal here is not to be a Gift Grabber and get European guys to buy you things; it's to let them meet you in the chivalrous manner that they prefer.

If after you spend the time to meet and learn about Mr. Drink Buyer you find that he is a mismatch, a smile and appreciative words are sufficient. If he is a home run, then the drink is just the first base in your relationship.

Of course if there is a crowd all trying to order drinks, I wouldn't advise pausing before ordering yours. Not only will your future amour not have room to approach, but other possible candidates waiting to order will not get a good impression of you.

When I Learned the Beauty of Pausing

I learned this guy-meeting tip inadvertently. I often have a hard time deciding what to order—usually because the drink menu is full of such creative names. I mean, doesn't everyone know that a Barcelona Bay Blast is really a beverage with something like Everclear plus Sprite, strawberry-kiwi concentrate, and a twist of watermelon? Not so much. And since I don't drink alcohol—I'm with Jennifer Lopez, Jennifer Love Hewitt, and Blake Lively on this front—trying to say, "Could I please have a virgin Barcelona Bay Blast" is a total tongue twister and takes up time. One evening, my friend observed, "You always get offered drinks when you have a hard time deciding what to order. I've already got mine and started drinking it alone by the time some cute guy buys yours." After that, she started pausing when ordering and met several men.

Tip #28:
The Last Sips of Your Drink Are Pivotal

If you did not get the chance to pause while ordering your drink or your future European hunk did not seize his opportunity to meet you, don't despair. Once you have your drink in hand, you have another shot at meeting men. The last sips of your drink are pivotal. Swallow them slowly while leisurely walking around so that the men can notice you and the fact that your drink is getting low. This gives them the perfect chance to offer to buy you another one and become better acquainted.

Tip #29:
Top It Off at Tipsy

If you love your alcohol, consider giving the liver a rest while overseas. In many regions, Europeans are known for not drinking nearly as much as those from certain other countries—except at festivals, where all bets are off. So if you stumble about wasted, you will most likely be looked down on by the European men.

One of my girlfriends from college drinks to the max and beyond. She has the tolerance of a quarterback and exceeds it at least weekly. After ten shots, her dancing partner can range from a guy to a door jam. Frat boys found this hilarious, but when she went abroad the European men acted like she was a freak. After learning to top off her drinking at tipsy, she went from an alien to a spicy number in demand.

I asked the men about this phenomenon. They explained that visitors from some countries have been known to get drunk, shout annoyingly, and destroy property. Take my girlfriend Bar Wrecker and Hometown Honey from Tip #14, Don't Cling to Men from Your Own Country. That man definitely did not top it off at tipsy and ended up shattering a lamp. I realize that this is a drastic example, but a few bad examples have given travelers from some nations a bad name. So it's better to just let European prospects know that public destruction is not in your dating plan by topping it off at tipsy.

Tip #30:
Make the Men Look at
Your Sexiest Dance Move

Not every girl is Julianne Hough and can look sexy doing every dance move. Seriously, she would probably be a stunner doing the lawn mower! Fortunately, that is not a criterion for European guy getting. All you need are one or two enticing dance moves and the ability to follow the Man-Meeting Dance Floor Formula. My girlfriends and I love to go clubbing in Europe. We perfected this five-step guy-attracting science. Here it is:

Man-Meeting Dance Floor Formula

Step 1: As you enter the dance floor, scan the room for male potential.

Step 2: Strategically place yourself near your target.

Step 3: Keep glancing at him until he looks at you.

Step 4: Encouragingly smile.

Step 5: Look away and dance one of your best moves.

Remember, if you only have one sexy dance move, no big deal. Your European man doesn't have to know this now. The point is to get him to approach you and be enchanted by your fun personality. If you have more dance tricks up your sleeve, that's great. If your potential date does not approach, you may have to look back and smile again. Like I said, European men usually don't need much encouragement.

If something goes astray in your execution of the formula and the outcome is not what you anticipated, the solution could be in the next tip.

Tip #31:
Use Dancing with the Girls
to Attract the Guys

Have you ever entered a club filled with appealing chaps who were glued to the wall? Stepping onto the dance floor seemed off of their agendas. My girlfriends and I have faced this predicament. We've tried everything from casually walking by them, to introducing ourselves, to even flat-out asking them to dance—but every time we were unsuccessful in plucking these male wallflowers.

When the Guys Stepped Away from the Wall

Then, on my fourth trip to Europe, I experienced the most drastic case of masculine wall-itis. My friend and I headed out to the hippest club in the city only to find the men stoically standing on the sidelines while the women congregated in the restroom, scheming about how to engage the fellas. Although the music was enticing, the dance floor was empty.

My spunky friend grabbed my arm and declared, "If those guys just want to stand and stare, we'll give them something to stare at." She led me to the center of the room and whispered, "Let the show begin!" We started dancing and she twirled me several times. It did the trick. The guys started looking in our direction. Once we captured their attention, my friend slowly spun me toward the two most stunning targets. We kept dancing until we were only a foot away from them. After glancing over our shoulders and smiling encouragingly, the Casanovas took a daring step away from the wall. Then they joined us on the dance floor.

Other friends have also used this tactic. We have never seen it fail! European men are attracted to confident women who show that they can have fun together even when the boys are being boring.

How to Handle Menacing Men

There will be times on your European trip when a wannabe heart-throb is coming on to you and you do not want his amorous advances. These are usually also the times when there is an enthralling man nearby whose acquaintance you definitely want to make. At those moments it is important to have mastered the art of Getting Rescued by a Gorgeous Guy (GRGG, pronounced like the guy's name).

Tip #32:
Getting Rescued by a Gorgeous Guy

There are two approaches to GRGG—passive and aggressive. The first doesn't even involve talking, while the second is a direct confrontation. Just do what makes you comfortable. If you are the type of gal who feels so ill at ease asking a guy to escort you someplace that you have to practice on your girlfriend a million times before popping the question, don't even think about going aggressive. I would know. I live on the passive path. The one time I tried to venture into aggressive land, I felt so silly that I started laughing. Then my mark got offended and left because he though I was laughing at him. Oops!

The passive approach is simply a pleading look directed at Mr. Hottie. If he is a catch, he will most definitely come and rescue a darlin' in distress. If he ignores your nonverbal SOS, be glad. You don't want to associate with someone who isn't willing to help out a gem like you.

When I Met Prince Charming Through Passive GRGG

My first experience with using the passive approach to GRGG was at a packed club. It was really hard to move and I was constantly being pushed. A man, let's call him Mr. Slimy, grabbed me and started dancing. He wanted to salsa, but refused to teach me the steps. So basically, I felt like a puppet being yanked around. To make matters worse, his rendition wasn't like any I had ever seen. I think he was trying to invent a new game called "Strip Salsa." I let Mr. Slimy know exactly how I felt about his traveling hands, but he didn't stop. I pushed through the crowd to get away from him, but he followed. My girlfriend was happily involved with another man, so I couldn't escape to her.

Then I saw a stunning Frenchman—let's call him Mr. Prince Charming—standing on the other side of the floor. I flashed him a look that pleaded, "Come save me!" Two seconds later, Mr. Prince Charming shoved his way through the madding crowd and asked Mr. Slimy, "Can I steal her from you?" Mr. Slimy rudely replied, "Who do you think you are?" Mr. Prince Charming smoothly shot back, "The man who is about to steal the lady you are pestering." He led me to a table away from the crowd and we enjoyed a wonderful finish to what could have been a miserable night.

When the It Girl Met Mr. Greek God
Through Aggressive GRGG

The butterfly who received the title of "European It Girl" in Tip #12 never went for the passive scenario. The aggressive approach suited her personality, and her success rate always shot through the roof. A textbook example of this tactic occurred one afternoon while she was exploring a flea market. A creepy male leech wouldn't detach himself from her. She tried to kindly keep her distance, but every time she moved to another booth, Mr. Leech moved right beside her. Then she spotted Mr. Greek God. She instantly ran up to him, pretended that he was a long-lost friend and proclaimed, "Wow, what a surprise! I haven't seen you in years." Without pausing, she turned back to Mr. Leech and politely explained, "This is an old friend of mine. It was nice meeting you." As Mr. Leech left, the European It Girl winked at Mr. Greek God and said, "Thank you so much for saving me." As she turned to leave, her walking wonder winked back and said, "Wait. Shouldn't old friends catch up over lunch?" She dated him for the next couple of weeks while she was in the city—that is, among her dates with other European men. She was a NCD (Non-Committal Dater) all the way.

How to Deal with the Do's and Don'ts of Dining

Dining probably seems pretty simple—I mean we do it every day. But in Europe, how a lady acts while enjoying a meal with a European man can determine whether she will get asked out again. The first tip in this section addresses formal dining etiquette, which can vary from area to area. The other tips let you in on the secrets of the often unspoken—but always pertinent—dining habits that can make a date sizzle or fizzle.

Tip #33:
Use Etiquette as an Icebreaker

So you meet a mesmerizing man at a club, on the slopes, or reveling in the throngs at a festival. You find yourself so taken that the hours just slip by. He asks you out on a dinner date the next evening. Great! But somehow when you get there, conversation doesn't seem to come as naturally as it did the night before. The love potion has not worn off. It's just that you didn't have to talk that much while dancing, schussing side-by-side enthralled with the snowy scenery, or enjoying the fireworks sweeping above the festival.

When you are sitting across the table from each other without any of these pleasant distractions, your nerves can take center stage and an awkward silence can set in. Then, even if your date gets two thumbs up for looks, staring into his eyes will get old after a couple of minutes. Some simple icebreaking questions can jumpstart the evening. Once you and your companion relax and you get him to open up, conversation should again become easy. It is normally just the first ten minutes that prove problematic.

I found that asking a date about his country's dinner etiquette is a perfect conversation-opener. Table manners vary in different areas and I was surprised to learn that something perceived as impolite at home could be a sign of relishing your meal abroad. For example, when dining with a Spaniard, I was told that it was preferable to rest my forearms on the table.

So not only is it important to get the info on dining must-do's, but doing this on a date is a good way to flatter your European dinner mate by letting him know that you want to make a good impression and learn about his culture. It will also help him warm up as he happily becomes your etiquette teacher.

THE BOTTOM LINE

You really don't need to do extensive prior research on dining etiquette before embarking on a pleasure trip, since learning

> it from your European man is the ideal icebreaker. On the other hand, if your trip abroad is business oriented, you'd better brush up on etiquette before boarding the plane.

Tip #34:
Picky Never Was Sexy

Shrimp with the heads and eyes still attached and baby veal may seem like ample cause to stick up your nose and ask for tofu or a hamburger. Don't! No European man wants to take you on a date, introduce you to his home specialties, and have you wrinkle up your forehead in disgust. Take a deep breath, glance the other way, chew, swallow, and smile. You will probably find that these delicacies are actually quite delicious. I did, and I used to be the queen of picky. If you don't like them, be an actress. Compliment what you do like, but don't say anything demeaning about the rest.

When I Professed My Love for Ketchup and Didn't Get Love Back

Drenching an unpleasant taste—or anything for that matter—in ketchup is a major no. I found this out when I was on my first European dinner date. I absolutely adore ketchup. I put it on almost everything from calamari to peas. So when the handsome Hungarian sitting across from me ordered lobster, I didn't think twice about asking the waiter to hand over the Heinz. And yes, I was quite happy that the restaurant even had my favorite brand in little individual bottles.

My dashing date didn't look pleased. He explained that the chef was preparing other wonderful sauces. Not getting the hint, I happily professed my love for ketchup and let the waiter bring it to the table. The meal was perfect, but I couldn't understand why I suddenly felt like I was conversing with a statue. Then the bill came. Fuming, my new European honey signed the check while muttering, "I paid a fortune for ketchup." A second date was not in the stars, but I never made this mistake again.

Tip #35:
No Man Wants to Date a Mouse

Many females have the reputation of picking away at their salads while refusing to touch any dressing that's not low fat. Really girls, if you fit this description, pretty please with sugar on top, cease and desist. European men are very turned off by women who push the food around on their plates while only occasionally taking a few bites. On a dinner date, having a hearty appetite is a key component in being asked out again.

I have a friend who barely reaches five feet and has a waistline that only seems as big as my little finger. Somehow she manages to down three appetizers, steak, pasta, and dessert like it's nothing. There just has to be a hole in her foot where all the food immediately exits! Guys thought she was absolutely adorable and wanted to take her out all the time. They bragged to their friends about how she could out-eat anyone. If you don't have the appetite of an elephant like my little friend, I'd advise eating light in the hours leading up to your date. That way you can get the maximum value out of your meal and many male returns.

When a Healthy Appetite Scored a Date
to the Society Ball

I learned the importance of not eating like a mouse one day while eavesdropping in a European park. I love people watching and picking up valuable tidbits. While enjoying my gelato next to a group of local guys, I honed in on their conversation. They were deliberating over who to ask to the high society event that was quickly approaching. Apparently this was quite the process. They seemed to analyze more girls than Europe has hot spots. Some of the deal breakers had to do with food. When various names were mentioned the men's responses ranged from, "No way. I took her to the nicest seafood restaurant in town and she ordered some lettuce. I could have just dropped her off at the grocery store," to "Like I want to spend an entire evening with a girl who leaves three-fourths of her plate untouched while the rest of us are enjoying ourselves."

 MAN-MEETING TIDBIT. I also learned that although European gentlemen want their ladies to eat ample amounts, wolfing down dinner in mere moments won't win you another invite. Chew slowly. Pause between portions to revel in your exotic encounter. Europeans are notorious for taking their time to savor the sauces and spices. And believe me, you will want to. Food seems to taste so much better in Europe, especially when you are enjoying it with an amazing guy.

Tip #36:
Avoid Packing on Those Pesky Pounds

You do want to eat to impress, but porking up is never fun. Then your clothes won't fit and going naked is not a viable alternative. Granted, you will attract attention, but after you have been cuffed and thrown behind bars, the only prospects will be your jail mates. A good compromise is to continue eating but amp up the exercise. It's quite easy to do that in Europe with so many beautiful scenes. Take a morning run or an evening stroll, incorporate biking or climbing into your vacay, or increase the nights of the week that you go dancing. All of this does wonders for keeping off those pesky pounds.

When I Learned to Savor the Sauces
and Still Fit My Cute New Clothes

I committed the creeping weight mistake the first time I went to Europe. All the food was so delicious, and I wanted to make every moment memorable. I sure did! Starting early in the morning after my Rouen omelet, I'd stop by the neighborhood bakery. Two pineapple tarts really didn't do the chef justice, so I'd take a raspberry one for the road. I'd enjoy it at noon, accompanied by sparkling cider, while checking out the guys. Lunch was always a landmark. The cafés served foot-long toasted treats. Why eat a simple sandwich when you can order chocolate paradise on a plate as the appetizer to roasted duck with cherries? But dinner was the real ticket. The bars offered fresh-cut braised pork right off the skewer. A pound of juicy meat and veggies drenched in butter, then back on over to the bakery for a peach crepe was the best way to wrap up the day.

After about a week of this overindulgence, I couldn't zip up my new dress. Yikes! I didn't want to cut out all the chow, so I started replacing some sugary snacks with local options that were lower on the food pyramid. I also increased my amount of clubbing and began walking through the rose garden every evening—that is, after my last bakery visit. The extra pounds quickly melted away and I was able to wear all my cute new clothes instead of just slipping on sweatpants. From then on, I made sure to keep those molecules moving, the endorphins flowing, and the extra pounds off.

Many of the hot spots described in this guide are actually cardio builders. While you take in the European men, you can let go of the extra calories.

How to Have the Most Fun Dating Foreigners

You may be in Europe for just a week and only get to slip in a sprinkling of dates. You may be staying for months and desire a serious European relationship. Or, since this is singles' paradise, you may want to date around. Whatever you prefer, it is valuable to know the tips in this section. They not only help you have fun, they keep you safe.

Tip #37:
The First Date

If you're a visitor on unfamiliar turf and have just been asked out on a delightful-sounding date, be cautious until you get to know and trust your new companion. For the first date, it is smart to meet a man in a public place or plan a double date with a friend you have faith in. By taking these precautions, you're also paving the way to having your hottie pour on the princess treatment in order to convince you that he is an upstanding guy. I incorporated this rule into my travel repertoire after seeing what happened on a European road trip.

When Miss Intelligent Intrigued Mr. Scientific Sexpot

My very intelligent girlfriend was asked out by a charismatic, high-level engineer. She agreed with enthusiasm, but explained that she would feel much more comfortable if I came along on their first rendezvous. She suggested a double date, so Mr. Scientific Sexpot gladly invited his intriguing friend for me, and a goofy, hilarious guy that we nicknamed Gafas (see Types of European Men on page 110). We met these men at this charming candlelit restaurant on the beach. Since there were so many mouthwatering options on the menu, they ordered one of everything for us to try!

Not only did we have an excellent experience, but my friend's new amour continued courting her. He flew back early from the Paris Air Show to say good-bye before she left town, and now that she is home he is already planning a visit to the States. They talk every morning over Skype and email daily. She read me part of his last email. It said, "Por todo mi ser quiero besarte." This means, "With all of my being I want to kiss you." It sounds like we have a Spanish Shakespeare on our hands. My friend thinks he is the man of her dreams.

Tip #38:
"Thank You"—The Two Most Important Words in Any Language

If you had a fabulous time on your first European date—or any date for that matter—and want to reunite with your foreign find, you must grasp the magical impact of two little words: "Thank you."

When I Endeared Myself to
Mr. Romantic Party Thrower

I learned the power of thanking on a date with a Danish finance exec. I had been out with him a couple of times and knew that he was not only a great guy and a great numbers cruncher, but a great party thrower as well. He told me that he was planning a fancy party that weekend at his home and asked me to be his date. This was no average open house. All the ladies wore cocktail dresses and the men suits. His place was beautifully decorated. My romantic party thrower said he wanted everything to be perfect. It was, until one female guest became a little too smitten with the bartender—he was pretty cute—and drank too much wine.

The lady started acting inappropriately, hitting on other guests' dates, bumping into furniture, and distracting band members so that they played wrong notes. The Danish host had her taken home. After that, the party went right back to being a romantic experience straight out of a Peder Severin Krøyer painting. I had the best time. I loved everything—my date, the décor, my dress.

When it was over, I pretended that the drunken girl episode never happened and thanked Mr. Romantic Party Thrower, mentioning all the positive aspects of the evening. Later he confessed that even though the inappropriate guest was just a snippet of the night, it concerned him. If I had not sincerely thanked him, he might not have felt comfortable asking me out again. So always remember to say thank you and get excited for further dates.

Tip #39:
Serious Dating

Since this is *The Single Girl's Guide to Meeting European Men*, not *The Single Girl's Guide to Seriously Dating European Men*, I'm only going to touch upon this subject. I have girlfriends who entered into serious relationships with Europeans. Some never ended and others ended unhappily and abruptly. If you are in Europe for an extended period of time and meet a native who makes you feel like the stars align when you are together, if he understands your cultural differences, you understand his, and you are both willing to compromise, you may deem him boyfriend or even husband material. Some of you may be thinking, "Like that would happen!" Read on naysayers . . . I know girls who are now happily married to their European men.

Let's say that this keeper claims he has deep feelings for you. How do you know that he truly is a keeper? The **European Male Commitment Test** (EMCT) is practically foolproof in finding the answer. It has been used by several of my friends contemplating serious relationships with European men. Here it is:

The European Male Commitment Test

EMCT #1. When you are alone with your European man, does he:

A. Express the desire to date you and only you, and then ask how you feel about him? Is all of this done on his own initiative, without any coaxing on your part?

B. Express the desire to date you and only you, and then tell you what a nice ass you have?

C. Never bring up the desire to date you and only you?

Answer Analysis. A) By expressing his desire for an exclusive relationship and then asking your feelings, your European sweetie is showing that he not only cares about being with you, but also about what you want. B) Beware if the answer is any form of B. Your man is not stopping to ask about your feelings. He is just buttering you up because he wants to get some ass. What should you do? CYA (Cover Your Ass) and move on . . . that is, if you don't want to be "official" for a short amount of time and then get the DO-YA. C) Of course, all single girls know that C is never a good sign.

EMCT #2. When you ask to meet his friends, does he:

A. Make up excuses for why you can't?

B. Proudly introduce you to many of his friends?

C. Only introduce you to a handful of his friends?

Answer Analysis. A) You know this is bad. He could very well be keeping you from his friends because he is seeing another girl. B) By proudly introducing you to many of his friends as the girl he is dating, he is letting the people who mean the most to him know that he cares about you. C) Don't fall into this trap. He could only be showing you to a few friends because he is not ready to announce to the world that he is dating you.

EMCT #3. When you ask about his family, does he:

A. Skirt the issue?

B. Say very little?

C. Invite you to meet them? Or, if they do not live nearby, tell you as much as you want to know about them?

Answer Analysis. A and B are usually bad. If he skirts the issue or does not say much, you know there is something wrong in his relationship with his family. The ideal is to find a man who is not only nice to his mom, but loves her, and whose parents treat each other with love and respect. This is a good indication that he will love you and be nice to you. If his parents are divorced, watch how he treats his mother. Answer C is usually good. Inviting you to meet his family shows that a man is happy to let his family know that he is dating you.

EMCT Case Studies. If the answers to the three questions on the EMCT are A, B, and C, then you should have the ABCs for the foundation of a great serious relationship. Here are some case studies:

> My one friend who did not have the ABCs of a serious relationship decided to go exclusive anyway. Her European boyfriend was forced into this commitment, only introduced her to a few of his friends, and treated his mom poorly. **Result: Bad Ending.** He dumped my friend just two weeks before she went home and she never heard from him again.
>
> My second friend did have the ABCs of a serious relationship. **Result: Happily Ever After.** They are now blissfully married.
>
> My third friend also had the ABCs of a serious relationship. **Result: Model Boyfriend.** They dated for six months while she was in Europe. He treated her superbly. When she left for home, they each decided that it would be best not to have a long-distance relationship, but he still calls and sends flowers. Now she will not date any guy who does not treat her as well as he does. She knows she deserves it. We all deserve it . . . Proceed with pride!

When Mr. Heavenly Talker Hooked Londrea

My fourth friend is the one that I want to focus on. She is currently in a serious relationship with a European man. Let's call her Londrea because about eighteen months ago she took a job in London. Londrea had made several short trips to Europe and had fantastic experiences filled with equally fantastic dates when she decided it was time for long-term European exposure. Not many weeks after arriving in the city she met a charming Brit with an equally charming accent. I can vouch for this 100 percent. In writing this guide, I talked to him on the phone and got his side of the story. I can tell you two things for sure. First, his accent is so romantic that it makes you practically melt when you hear him. And second, he is totally head-over-heels taken with my friend.

On their third date, Londrea discovered that Mr. Heavenly Talker had serious relationship potential. Both of them are climbing experts, so he set up a weekend climbing trip about five hours away. Several of his closest friends who knew the area well and had guide maps promised to meet them there. They were planning on sharing a large tent so that Londrea could get to know Mr. Heavenly Talker without feeling uncomfortable or unsafe.

Good Start. He wanted to introduce this girl to his friends. Well, the "wanted to" was all that happened. Mr. Heavenly Talker picked Londrea up at her house and drove her to the campground, but none of his friends were anywhere to be found. There had been a miscommunication and my friend and Mr. Heavenly Talker were left with no guide map and a huge tent for just the two of them to share over the entire weekend.

Time to Get Cozy. Now you might say, "Sly move, Mr. Heavenly Talker!" Well, he may have been a charmer, but he was definitely no sly mover. He was quite shy. From talking with him, I can assure you that he never planned for his friends to not show. I could practically hear him blushing on the phone when he recounted the experience. Londrea was definitely not a loose girl, so she was quite worried that this would be *awkward*. She had nothing to fear. It was only awkward for the first couple of minutes, until she realized that she had so many interests in common with Mr. Heavenly Talker and they were such a perfect pair that they could have shared that tent for a year and still wanted more time together . . . maybe a slightly smaller tent though.

Meeting Mom. That weekend they discovered a lot of new climbing routes and a lot about each other. On their last night, Mr. Heavenly Talker said that his mother lived a short drive from the campground, that he had promised to drop by, and that he would love to have Londrea meet her. When they arrived at his mom's house, he made dinner for her and Londrea. So not only did he treat his mom royally, but he also proved that his cooking skills were as heavenly as his accent. What a third date—finding that they were the only ones sharing a ten-person tent, climbing without a map, meeting her new amour's mom, and having him cook for her!

In a Relationship. That was the beginning of a serious dating relationship. It has been over a year since then, Londrea has met all of his friends, and Mr. Heavenly Talker continues to treat her and his mom with love and respect. Practically every weekend, he takes Londrea on a romantic getaway. Last weekend they went climbing in Wales and stayed in a beautiful cottage. They have the ABCs of a serious relationship that should go down in the history of European love!

Tip #40:
Leaving Europe

It's time to go home. You don't want to part with all of your exciting local gents. You are already suffering from separation anxiety. Your body is boarding the plane while your mind is back with your native sweethearts dancing around the bonfires, skiing all the way into a nightclub, hiking down relationship lane, sipping a drink in an old palace, and enjoying all the exotic escapades that can only be experienced in Europe. Look on the bright side. You may get to see these guys and make that magic happen again. Many of my girlfriends who thought they were kissing the land of E good-bye forever have received tickets back. One got offered an opportunity to complete her master's degree in Spain on a full scholarship, another got an advertising job in Denmark, and a third got an airplane ticket from a European pastime who couldn't put her out of his mind. When saying your parting remarks, make sure to exchange email addresses. You never know what will happen. I have had the privilege of returning to Europe several times, and I was glad to have contacts.

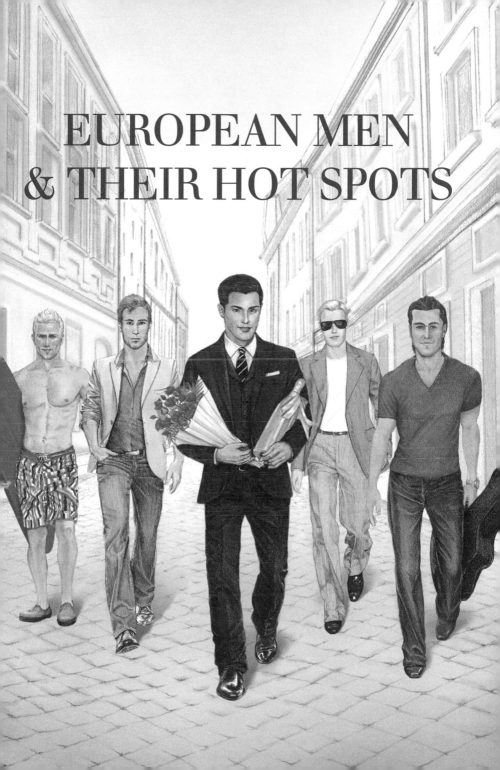

EUROPEAN MEN
& THEIR HOT SPOTS

Types of European Men

European males are not Stepford Men cast in certain molds. Each is uniquely different; however, there are ten general categories that can help you get a feel for the male possibilities. Well, technically there is an eleventh: "Jerks." But I'm leaving them off the official list because we aren't going to waste our assets on them when we can meet the men who are excited to meet us. Honestly, at all the places I went combined I could only count the number of jerks I met on one hand. They were like an endangered species. Now on to the male categories, starting with the A's.

About Business

These businessmen are successful entrepreneurs, doctors, engineers, writers, advertising execs, bankers, photographers, or consultants. They are not only about business, they are about having fun. During the workweek, these men are so busy handling important deals, surgeries, or accounts that you probably won't find them out on the town. But when the weekend comes, they want to unwind and meet single girls. Their motto: Party hard, work harder. You can find them anywhere from a hike to a swanky lounge. As for nightlife, About Businessmen normally only enter top-rung establishments. They have stimulating conversations and plan out everything, from the best PowerPoint presentations for convincing their clients to the best way to meet single girls, and the best places to take them on special dates. So if you want guys who have a plan, seek the About Business.

Airbrushed

These men have absolutely flawless features with seemingly no effort. Their interests and personalities vary and they can fall into any category—like Airbrushed About Business, Airbrushed Artsy, etc. The common denominator in these stunners is that whether they are thirteen or thirty-nine, they look so gorgeous that you won't be able to look away. Last week, I was seated on a plane next to a fifteen-year-old girl who had just met a bunch of European boys at camp. She summed it up exactly when she declared, "Even the thirteen-year-olds had six packs. And they stuffed in the food as if they were huge football players. I mean, aren't thirteen-year-old boys supposed to be gangly?" Supposed to be? Yes. Are they? Not even close! And if the thirteen-year-olds have six packs, you can only imagine what the twenty- and thirty-somethings have!

I love Airbrushed males and consider this quality a bonus, but for me it is not a requirement. What matters is that I am drawn to a man and enjoy his company. One night in Europe, I met someone who I thought was marvelous. My traveling companion said he wasn't attractive enough. Friends, there isn't such a thing as not attractive enough when a guy has all the right assets. If you are smitten with someone, don't let critics turn you away.

Artsy

These guys know everything about art. They can hold a conversation ranging from the spicy gossip about the top theater directors in town to the dissection of Mozart's chords. If you like lads who will tell you romantic love stories, it's not difficult to snatch a ticket into their hearts. You can meet them at any theater, concert, or art-influenced festival in any European country.

Artsy Man Lingo. If this type of guy asks you to come to his place to "listen to classical music" after watching a play and sharing wine and cheese, he does not just have listening to classical music in mind. My girlfriend can attest to this. She was extended such an offer by an Artsy. She soon discovered that the classical music was simply a ploy. Just because these guys are into art does not mean they don't have the moves. In fact, they have attended so many plays and concerts that to them pursuing you is a production in which they choreograph every romantic step.

Charismats

These gents are naturally suave and witty without seeming like they are putting on a show or trying hard to impress you. They were born with the charming gene. At a table with a group of European men, the Charismats will always catch your ear with their funny jokes. With them, you will be laughing a lot, but not the way you would with Gafas, who are described next. Charismats are not at all goofy. They can also take on different characteristics. I dated a distinctively About Business Charismat.

Gafas

These kinds of guys are fun and goofy. Having them around is always a delight. *Gafas* in Spanish means "eyeglasses." I named this category in honor of the first charming jokester I met in Europe. He wore these awesome quirky glasses (see Tip #37) and joined my girlfriend and me on a double date. He was what you would technically call the third wheel, but it didn't feel like that at all. He was the main enter-tainment of the evening—constantly cracking us up even though we were at a lavish restaurant, but never inappropriate. I wish I could have stayed in the city longer because I wanted to set up my zany girlfriend with this goofy fun guy. Well, there is always another trip to Europe for that. Gafas can be extremely successful, so you can find About Business Gafas, but these guys usually don't fall into categories like Artsy or Rock Star.

Groovers

These groovy guys are phenomenal dancers. The ones who aren't studying at conservatories are normally performing in music videos or participating in international dance competitions. It seems that dance is a lot more prevalent in Europe than in other parts of the world. Each Groover has his own specific personality. Just like Airbrushed and Charismats, Groovers can be hybrids, like Artsy Groovers, or the triple threat, Artsy Airbrushed Groovers! Mooching Groovers is one category, however, that does not exist, because Groovers are industri-ous and ambitious.

You can find Groovers at many top clubs. They enjoy trying out new moves in stimulating social environments, and they are gener-ally friendly with all types of dancers from experts to non-Groovers. I learned this at a salsa club filled with professionals. They were so awe-provoking that the dance floor looked like the stage at a *So You Think You Can Salsa* finale taping. My friends and I had a wide range of dancing skills. One could salsa but her ability was nowhere near the level of these experts, and another had two left feet. We were happy just watching the "performance." After a while, the Groovers noticed that we weren't dancing. They invited us to join them on the floor and acted equally as happy to dance with my friend who knew the steps as the one who had a hard time not tripping over her feet. Of course, men from some countries are known for being more hospitable than others.

Moochers

This is one type of guy to stay away from. Moochers are unemployed and live with their parental units way into adulthood, if not forever. If you meet a Moocher, move on before he mooches off of you. Unfortunately, this breed can be found anywhere. If Daddy pays for him to enter a swanky club or the country's best restaurant, he won't exactly need to be pushed through the door.

So here is the **Mooching Detector**: Ask the suspect what he does for a living. If the answer is, "I'm a club celeb," the translation is, "I use my parent's money to hang out at the clubs every night." If he says, "I'm in between jobs," you have to wonder if his last job was, oh, say . . . never. And if he gives you the clincher "I work for the family business," he may be telling the truth or, if he is a Moocher, he means, "My parents run the family business while I reap the rewards."

The problem with Moochers is that they often want you to pamper them just like their parents do. Don't rationalize by thinking, "Moochers are just Smoochers without the S." Not even close!

Outdoor Sports Aficionados

These outdoor hunks have the most enviable bodies. But our job isn't to envy them, it's to enjoy them! They typically have laid-back personalities but intense athletic motivation. Their three major loves: sports, the environment, and single girls. So go green and get these guys.

Outdoor Sports Aficionados include bikers, who are known for being neat and tidy and having amazing leg muscles and the best butts. (If you are going to meet them, take to heart Tip #26: Avoid the Bubble Butt.) Then there are the hikers, skiers, snowboarders, surfers, kiteboarders, connoisseurs of a variety of exotic extreme sports, and the *They Rock*—yep, those are the rock climbers! The snowboarders and surfers are the most radical partiers. They live on the edge and seek the thrill of adventure. In Europe, surfers are considered the snowboarders of the water. These nightlife hounds will often hit the bars after a day of working out while the They Rock love to hang . . . not just on the rocks, but around the campsites. It is an art form that you sports babes will want to embrace in order to meet them.

Rock Stars

There are two types of Rock Stars, Collegiate and Not-So-Collegiate, and the differences between them extend to more than their music.

Collegiate Rock Stars. This category contains the scholarly with a slightly edgy look. They often attend prestigious music conservatories, teach music at universities, or perform in symphonies . . . but they play in rock or the latest pop bands on the side, and that is their passion. They not only know how to read music, but are also generally quite the linguists, conversing in about six different languages. This is because they like to study languages and practice them when they perform with their bands in different countries. If you are looking for someone who has the sophistication to blend in to high society in a tux yet has the capability to hold his own in a jam session wearing an ironic T-shirt and jeans, here is your man. The Collegiate Rock Stars love the guitar, but are also adept at wind and brass instruments. The latter builds up mouth muscles, making these men not only Rock Stars, but creative Kissing Stars. They are fabulous!

Not-So-Collegiate Rock Stars. These men range from famous protégés who received record deals at young ages, to almost-famous musicians, to those trying to be famous and far from the mark. Depending on the type of music, the stage of his career, and the guy, there are a wide variety of Not-So-Collegiate Rock Stars. Just because they have not gone to college does *not* mean they aren't smart. Many of them are geniuses who would rather spend their time pursuing record deals than perusing textbooks. My girlfriends who are Rock Star connoisseurs unanimously claim that the downside of dating the Not-So-Collegiate types is that some are not as good at kissing as the Collegiate ones. That's because the Not-So's are often not so into playing the wind and brass instruments. Instead, they focus on the guitar. But who says that with a little encouragement they can't start exercising those mouth muscles on other instruments?

Slightly Sleazy

These guys treat partying like it is a career path. They are not Moochers because they do support themselves, but they believe in postponing sleep to hit the nightlife now. Slightly Sleazy men are often entertaining, nice guys, but they put a new meaning on the phrase "lovin' the single girls." They want to be all over you. Actually, they will do more than "want to" if given the chance. Caressing is their extracurricular activity. So if you are a gal who does not have a personal bubble and welcomes PDA, you can handle the S's. But if you feel like you need a shower the second you meet a Slightly Sleazy, politely pull away. He might try to draw you in once more, but most of these men are well meaning, so if you turn him down again he should leave you alone.

A Slightly Sleazy can be found anywhere, although you will be less likely to spot one in posh neighborhoods and at elite events. They like bars, certain clubs, and sports. Say a Slightly Sleazy was rock climbing and a single girl caught his eye. He would probably approach saying, "You look like you need some help." He would definitely give her a hand, but it would be by boosting her up under the butt. If this freaks you out and a Slightly Sleazy won't leave you alone, see Tip #32: Getting Rescued by a Gorgeous Guy.

Now that you are in on the different types of European men, it's time to learn the hot spots where you can find them!

The Hottest Spots to Meet European Men

Each of the following countries begins with an overview of attractions followed by a list of tried-and-true man-meeting venues. The guy-getting tips you learned in the first part of this book will work anywhere you find a sufficient supply of testosterone, but in the listed venues single girls have found the mother lode.

Just as different girls like different types of activities, different locations draw in different types of European males. Personally, I don't discriminate. I'm attracted to many kinds of guys—from About Business to Outdoors Sports Aficionados to Rock Stars. Some of the locations on my list are hidden secrets that you will not want to miss. Others are local hangouts that tourists can inadvertently pass by. Of course, no one can foretell which male will cross your path at any location, and we all realize that on any given day the man-meeting conditions in any given place can vary, but I am confident that you will enjoy yourself at each of these destinations and up your chances of meeting eligible European men. So choose the places and activities that sound most appealing to you. Then go prowling!

At most venues, you will encounter a variety of European men. Some attract more of one type than another. If that is the case, I will clue you in. Also, at each landmark, you can encounter men from a variety of nations. Europeans often travel from one country to another to work, intern, attend school, or vacation. In fact, when I lived in London for two months, I met more Swedes, Swiss, and Spaniards on average than I did Brits . . . so you will have plenty of opportunities to find the guys you are looking for.

Word to the Dining Wise. Many of these venues are known for serving alcohol and caffeinated coffee and tea. If you're the type whose beauty and health regimen does not include these beverages, don't assume you have to cut yourself out of the fun. European eateries provide enticing alternatives.

Austria

Austria is famous for snow sports, *The Sound of Music*, and Mozart. The Alpine region is dotted with ski villages. The most-visited and fanciest winter-sport resorts are found in Kitzbühel. For ladies who lend themselves to highbrow culture, Austria hosts classical festivals and concerts in grand castles and on lakes with floating stages, plus a Vienna ball season. For those into pop culture, some of the best nightlife is also in Vienna . . . and in Salzburg, St. Pölten, and Graz, where college students compose one fourth of the population. There are plenty of opportunities to hone your man-meeting skills in all those places, but the following Alpine area has been proven to produce an avalanche of lust-worthy males.

Saint Anton (MooserWirt)

Saint Anton, located at the end of the Arlberg pass, is the sporty Alpine center for seamlessly combining skiing or snowboarding with partying. Experts and adrenaline junkies will love the Valluga gondola, which climbs to a series of runs from the center of the resort. On the edges are the bunny hills and in between are intermediate runs.

When Miss Newbie Won the Guy-Getting Race

One of my girlfriends experienced the entire spectrum of skiing difficulty on her first ski trip ever. It is one of the most unique European man-meeting stories I know. She went skiing with some relatives who were experienced. One of them was a cousin her age with a mischievous streak. Miss Mischievous got Miss Newbie outfitted and took her to the top of a hill, promising to give her a lesson. She got her all lined up, facing downhill, grasping her poles with her skis clamped on—and then she shoved her. She called that a lesson? Well, she had the "less" part right. She had less of her cousin to deal with while Miss Mischievous turned her attention to hitting on the men. But they didn't even notice her while staring at Miss Newbie heading straight down the hill like a bullet with her skis in a perfect, tight parallel position. She had done a little waterskiing and had pretty good balance, but she had never skied on snow before and had no idea how to use her equipment.

Skiers started calling out to those around her, warning them to get out of the way. Those in front of her scrambled to escape, glancing back with a look of sheer terror. Before she got going so fast that everything became a blur, Miss Newbie saw a member of the ski patrol ahead of her and tried to follow him, thinking this was her safest way out. Suddenly, he became airborne. She soon learned that he had gone over a jump as she went over the same one. She saw a chalet looming ominously in front of her and did not know how to avoid emulating a Road Runner and Coyote cartoon, with her image etched in it, so she sat down for several yards—the butt stop. She finally quit moving when she was only a foot from the side wall.

Some Austrian guys helped her up, told her they had seen everything, and invited her to ski with them. She could not have had more expert instruction or more delightful company. They spent the day guiding her through increasingly difficult runs and taking turns help-ing her over the hardest parts. As she neared the end of the last run, she saw her mischievous cousin ski straight into the same chalet wall. And this was without a European man by her side!

MooserWirt—For Those in the Know. Despite the happy ending, Miss Newbie does not recommend this tactic for meeting European men, but she does recommend going to MooserWirt if you visit Saint Anton and can hold your own as a skier. MooserWirt is a club in the middle of the slope where the Outdoor Sports Aficionados flock (+43 (0) 5446-3588). Ladies, if you like men with nice muscles, grab those skis. This is not for the pink and squishy. The only way to get to the club is by taking the gondola to the top of the run and skiing halfway down. Get excited to see the A+ athletes shake it on top of the tables while still wearing their snow boots. Hop on up there and join them. The golden rule of MooserWirt is, "Dance atop the tables for sexy male skiers as you would have sexy male skiers dance atop the tables for you." After all, this is what the club is known for.

This must-stop opens during the day and is known for staying cranked-up until well after the sun sets. When you are done drink-ing and munching back all those calories you burned off while ski-ing down the first half of the slope, say farewell to MooserWirt and glide the rest of the way down. If you leave after dark, you will want a headlight, because the route is pitch black. And this is one time to really adhere to the top-it-off-at-tipsy rule. For those who overin-dulge, passing out and spending the night on cold snow will make a hangover that much worse.

This hot spot is not known for staying open late at night, so if you are a hardcore partier, think of MooserWirt as your rambunctious fun pre-gaming. Then finish your night in town at one of the several hopping party haunts.

Fashion Flash. Kühl is the cool brand to wear in Saint Anton. With this hip outdoor attire, the Austrians will know that you are not only serious about snow sports but on top of their trends.

Belgium

Belgium is known for having so much medieval architecture and atmosphere that you'll feel like a time traveler. Brussels and Antwerp are its vibrant cities. In the summer, Ghent, a medieval canal city, hosts one of Europe's biggest festivals. It's free, and side festivals spring up every year with specialties like jazz, comedy, street theater, and electronic dance music. Ghent is also one of the biggest university towns in the country. With Belgium's environment, romance should be everywhere. Girls have been especially successful at finding it in Brussels' Delirium Café.

Brussels (Delirium Café)

Are you an aspiring artist who wants to meet Rock Stars? Do you love to be onstage? Are your musical talents amazing? If the answers to these questions are yes, yes, and yes, Delirium Café is the best outlet for you to show off your repertoire and mesmerize the males.

This stop is located at Impasse de la Fidélité, 4A, 1000 Bruxelles (+32 (0) 2-514-4434). Mostly macho men stream into this joint—not just once, but over and over again. Their goal is to try out all of the over two thousand beer selections. Yeah right! Like they can really guzzle all those drinks. But they will try to make you think that they can. Who cares? Go along with their bragging. Soothing the male ego plays a part in attracting the Delirium regulars.

The café is quite colorful inside. It is draped in—what do you know—boozing décor and situated along a little street with other novelty enclaves: an old bistro, a hub with pirate decorations, and an assortment of other bars. All partiers love the Delirium mascot. How can they not? It is a darling pink elephant prominently painted on the sign outside.

Back to you incredible musicians . . . Get looking good and head on over to the Delirium Café for one of the Thursday night jam sessions. They normally begin around 10 PM and are mainly testosterone fests. Don't just be one of the few females onstage; show up everyone with your musical expertise and cute coquettishness. While you are jamming away, look out into the audience and flash those pearly whites. Being treated like a music celeb onstage and flocked to afterward by admiring European men is the perfect end to this evening.

If you are not musically inclined, don't worry. I definitely fall into this category. I can't carry a tune and what I learned in Intro to Piano doesn't exactly present a wow feature during a jam session. If this is also your story, Delirium normally won't be as much of a guy-getting gig . . . but you never know. Read on!

When Miss Tone-Deaf's Musical Number Charmed the Men

One of my supreme guy-getting stories features a girlfriend who definitely can't carry a note . . . much less a tune. She traveled to Europe with some girlfriends who were stunning vocalists. Of course they took advantage of the jam fest. Miss Tone-Deaf's friends asked her to join them in the spotlight. At first she declined, but they kept asking until she agreed. She was just gracing the stage to be supportive and had no intention of singing. Lip-syncing and smiling was her plan. She had a lot of spunk, so the eyes in the room were really drawn to her. Afterward men surrounded her proclaiming, "You have the most incredible voice." When she responded, "Oh no, that was my friend standing next to me," they replied, "Don't be shy. We know a good voice when we hear one." She got many dinner offers and one suitor sent roses to her room.

THE BOTTOM LINE

Even if you're an amazing musician, be sure to have your spunk shining through and your guy-attracting glow on. Miss Tone-Deaf did and got more attention than her friends who actually had the singing chops. Unfortunately, they didn't get her the chaps.

Czech Republic

The Czech Republic is celebrated for its castles, ski resorts, and protected natural landscapes. There you'll find hiking and biking trails, rock climbing, and volcanic basalt rock formations that look like fingers. The historic city of Prague is the main point of entry into the country. It has some of the best shopping and coolest clubs. The top shopping streets are Na Prikope and Parizska. While you're checking out the fashions, check out the European men. My friends say that some of the premium places to meet them are in Prague's clubs.

When the Girls Learned That Bow Ties Are Hot

One of the best Czech man-meeting stories I have heard occurred one evening when a small group of girls arrived in Prague for the weekend. They couldn't speak Czech, couldn't read their Czech map, and couldn't find a restaurant to have dinner at before clubbing. While wandering around in a confused state, they were approached by a charismatic European man who spoke their language with a romantic accent. They nicknamed him "Bow Tie" because he was wearing one. Most guys could never pull it off, but Bow Tie was a Rock Star in a band and he could rock his red bow tie just as well as he could rock a jam fest. He gave the girls detailed directions to a "fabulous" restaurant and disappeared just as quickly as he had appeared. The girls were disappointed. During the walk to the restaurant they talked about how one of them should have gotten his number in case they "got lost again." Good one! These girls knew how to use getting lost to their man-meeting advantage.

At the restaurant, while the group waited for their table, they continued discussing the cute qualities of Bow Tie and how they wished he had come with them. Don't be too quick to make wishes in Prague . . . they tend to come true. One girl turned around to see Bow Tie himself standing right beside her. Surprise! He explained, "I just wanted to make sure that you found the restaurant." They shared a meal and he invited them to see him perform in concert.

So you can meet the European men in Prague pre-club as well as at the clubbing hot spots.

When Mr. Biz Gave Me the Lowdown on Czech Guys

My family and I are friends with a gentleman—let's call him "Mr. International Businessman" because he does business around the world. I have known him since I was four years old when he stayed at our house on a trip to Seattle. Now he is about seventy, but he is the funniest, hippest, most in-the-know seventy-year-old ever. A couple of months after he stayed with us he called asking to speak to my parents, but they weren't home. I answered the phone and we chatted for about an hour. Not many men can have that long of a conversation with a four-year-old as well as be in tight with everyone from kings and queens to presidents, put together business deals across the globe, and organize charity events everywhere for underprivileged kids. I honestly don't know how he does it all! He reminds me of the international businessman's version of Clint Eastwood.

Fifteen years ago, Mr. Biz bought a house in the Czech Republic and started living there part-time. When I told him that I was writing this book, he wanted the single girls to know that Prague has amazing clubs and that the local women love to dance, but most Czech men won't dance with them until they have downed enough liquid courage. You may be wondering how a seventy-year-old knows about clubbing. Well, he does business deals with locals in their twenties and thirties. Czech men love to party before, in the middle of, and after every business deal, so Mr. Biz has been to all of the top Czech clubs. He says it keeps him young and that the About Business guys are especially drawn to the hot spot Karlovy Lázně. At one of his first Prague clubbing experiences, he had to dance with all of the guys' girlfriends until they drank enough to get their groove on. Mr. Biz has a dry sense of humor, so he let the lads know that he expected them to pay him!

THE BOTTOM LINE

When you go clubbing in this country, be patient while waiting for the men to move themselves into dance mode. Think of it this way: In the Czech Republic, it doesn't take two to tango, it takes three—you, the guy, and Corona.

 MAN-MEETING TIDBIT. When I asked Mr. Biz if most Czech guys would be friendly to a traveling girl, he said, "If she is hot, you bet you!" So get yourself looking hot and head over to the following clubs.

Prague (Karlovy Lázně)

If you're into serious clubbing, don't miss Karlovy Lázne˘, which is right off of Charles Bridge at Smetanovo nábřeži 198, 110 00, Praha 1 (+420 222-220-502). You've already heard a testimonial from Mr. Biz.

Karlovy Lázně has the reputation as the largest dance club in Central Europe. There are actually five clubs within this club, each located on a different level. Here you should definitely be able to choose the dance style and European man you want. And Karlovy Lázně has a bonus for you architecture and history buffs. The interior of this club of clubs dates back to the 14th and 15th centuries, complete with original mosaics and preserved Roman-style spa pools—minus the water—that provide two of the dance floors.

Word to the Wise. The lines here are long on weekends. This is one of those times to faithfully follow the dressing tips in this guide. That just might get you escorted to the front.

Prague (Klub Lávka)

If you are passing through Prague in the summer, consider lighting at Klub Lávka, aka the Lávka Bar & Club, found on Novotného Lávka 1, Old Town, 110 00, Praha 1 (420 221-082-299; +420 221-082-278). This hot spot is next to the Charles Bridge on the edge of the Vltava river. It is open twenty-four hours a day and looks out at the city's castle.

On warm evenings, patrons pack onto the riverside terrace tucked away at the back of the bar. The view is magnificent, as are the dancing ladies who take turns strutting their stuff on the podium. I don't mean to be the bearer of bad news, but guys love cheering them on. This is why it's imperative that you stop by Pineapple Dance Studio on your way to Prague (see London Hot Spots on page 138). Fine-tuning the moves that make men's heads snap is your only saving grace.

Also, realize that Klub Lávka's hired dancers draw in gorgeous guys. On a typical night, 75 percent of the attendees are male. If you are an amazing dancer, coming here is a no-miss. Can you outdance the podium posse? If so, you should be destined for at least a dozen European dates!

Prague (Mecca)

This techno club is worth the trek into the depths of Prague to mingle with the city's best-looking guys. It is located on U Průhonu 3, 170 00, Praha 7 (+420 602-711-225). Who could have guessed that a converted warehouse in an industrial area would become such a big social draw?

For you girls who thrive on the glamour clubbing scene, Mecca is your home. Go all out—dress up, wear movie star makeup, do your nails, gloss your hair, and bronze the five highpoints. The bouncer will only accept the most attractive prospective attendees. So flaunt what you've got and believe in your appeal.

This hot spot is festively spiced up with colored lights and sparkling disco balls. The color spectrum revolves around bright pink, purple, and yellow. Wearing a dress or a sexy top with tasteful sequins will catch the light and set you apart from the other belles. You might even be mistaken for a member of the glitterati!

Word to the Wise. On certain nights, Mecca is especially swarming with studs. I would advise calling ahead to get the inside scoop. Only make your appearance when one of Mecca's best DJs is booked. This place is either feast or famine. You don't want to get all done-up for a disappointing turnout.

Denmark

Denmark may be best remembered for Copenhagen's Little Mermaid sculpture, but this is not the only lady celebrated by Danish men. You should find an appreciative audience when you practice your flirting tips on the guys in this capital city famous for its fashions and nightlife. Sportswomen can find men with interests close to their hearts congregating at soccer matches and sailing. Fashionistas flock to Copenhagen in February and August when it hosts Fashion Week, the largest style show in northern Europe. The party mood in this city begins in the evenings at the many cafés and bars. Around midnight it shifts to the clubs. One of Copenhagen's nightlife hubs is a car-free zone called Strøget. Its main attraction is Danish men. Another Danish city known for music and nightlife is Aalborg, "Little Paris of the North." One of its most popular streets is Jomfru Ane Gade, or "The Street."

Man-Meeting Tidbit. Danish men are more reserved than, say, Italian and Spanish males, but they love to meet single girls and are oozing with chivalry. I know that women have met charming Danes at the following destinations.

Copenhagen (Rust)

The club Rust is found at Guldbergsgade 8, København N. 2200 (+45 3524-5200). It is popular with Danish men and has three floors with a 670-person occupancy limit that I hear is usually at capacity. So you should find enough Danish guys there to meet your match. Rust is also known for quenching the clubaholic's jiving thirst and the music lover's desire for hot new artists. This venue has live music every Thursday, Friday, and Saturday, and sometimes other nights of the week. It often hosts up-and-coming talent. Many of the singers are from Copenhagen and are Collegiate and Not-So-Collegiate Rock Stars. You might just be able to snatch a future Danish celeb who can show you the inside European music scene.

Rust is where my girlfriend met the oh-so-attractive Danish gent who unfortunately didn't speak much English (and she didn't speak his language). They were the ones who managed to get through five dates while heavily relying on pantomiming (see Tip #19: Break Through Language Barriers). She met him while pausing to order her drink and didn't even have to wait around to take advantage of her last sips.

Word to the Wise. As much as Rust is known for being a prime lookout for Danish male sights, there won't be any sights to see on Monday, Tuesday, or Sunday. This haunt is normally only open Wednesday through Saturday.

My girlfriends have heard a lot of indie rock at this hot spot, but it also features other music genres, so go to www.rust.dk/pages/

koncerter.php to see the artist lineup when you will be in town. The band descriptions are in Danish under "Koncerter." Fortunately there are links to the acts' personal pages on social networking sites like Facebook, so you can check out the guys in the bands and get a sneak preview of their style to determine if you want to plan a Rock Star romance into your European trip.

Man-Admiring Tidbit. Rumor has it among rockin' chicks that the Danish band Mono Agenda has lust-worthy prospects performing at Rust. They say one member, Mikkel Aas, needs to replace the second letter of his last name with "s" and add the word "nice" before it. I realize that this guide has quite a focus on butts, between avoiding the DO-YA and the bubble butt and admiring the European soccer players' enviable rear ends (explanation upcoming), but this tip is not on me . . . Just thought you'd like to know the word among the SGA. Maybe Mono Agenda will perform again when you are at Rust so you can form your own opinion.

Copenhagen (Midsummer Night's Eve)

Summer Solstice or Midsummer Night's Eve celebrations occur throughout Europe during the longest day of the year, which usually falls between June 20 and 26. This tradition has been handed down from ancient times, and the celebration often involves bonfires and fireworks on the beach symbolizing the defeat of darkness by the conquering Sun God and the hope for a fertile harvest in the coming fall. In Denmark this festival is called Sankt Hans Aften, which means "the evening before the day of John the Baptist." You might be wondering why a protestant Christian country would follow a predominantly Catholic custom. Actually, the tradition predates the country's conversion to Christianity, which shows that the Danes are sentimental people who like to keep a connection with the past.

Bar Wrecker from Tip #14 can attest that Midsummer Night's Eve in Copenhagen draws in the men . . . especially not to miss are the Danish army officers. The festival takes place at the beach during the evening and night of June 23 and attracts throngs of Danes. They mingle, drink, and party. When they are done doing that, they drink and party some more. Hopefully by this point the dashing men have already found the single girls, so they have moved past the mingling stage to the getting-to-know-you scene. Don't cling to a guy from your own country at this celebration. Then, unlike Bar Wrecker, you can enjoy your Danish man while bypassing an awkward confrontation and a visit with your homeboy in jail!

MAN-MEETING TIDBIT. Music is an important part of Sankt Hans Aften. "Midsommervise," which means "Midsummer Song," is sung at every festival throughout Denmark. If you attend the event, impress your Danish target by knowing the words. If you really want to come off as a hip visitor, look up the band Shu-bi-dua. In 1979, they did a popular remake of the traditional song.

Caveat. There is one Danish Midsummer Night's Eve tradition that saddens some festivalgoers. Straw doll-like figures resembling witches are burned at beach bonfires reminiscent of witch burnings in the sixteenth and seventeenth centuries. A friend who attended this festival reported that Danish men told her they have changed the meaning of this tradition. In their hearts, they consider it symbolic of banishing evil spirits . . . Obviously a few evil spirits escaped when Hometown Honey smashed the lamp!

If you are uncomfortable watching these doll burnings, don't attend this festival. Your friends should understand. But if you can consider this ritual as simply a symbolic clearing of evil and a fresh start, then this is a great place to meet Danish men.

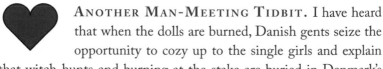 ANOTHER MAN-MEETING TIDBIT. I have heard that when the dolls are burned, Danish gents seize the opportunity to cozy up to the single girls and explain that witch hunts and burning at the stake are buried in Denmark's past. Many towns have even started a new festival tradition of burning the old to make way for the new. This is why Danish men think that the Midsummer Night's Eve is the perfect place to start a new relationship with a single girl.

Copenhagen (Tivoli)

This amusement park is a whole planet in and of itself located on Vesterbrogade 3, 1630 København V (+45 3315-1001). It contains twenty-one restaurants, twenty cafés and bistros, enormous firework displays, Friday rock concerts with bands playing on the Open Air Stage, and an assortment of other performances. That is just the tip of Tivoli's festive iceberg. There are a variety of tailor-made rides for all types of personalities, from wusses to daredevils. If you can muster the courage to step in line for the largest and most fear-provoking roller coaster thrills, you will automatically gain points with Copenhagen's gutsy males. They want to take the role of protector. Don't be surprised if your new admirer tries to pull you in close while free-falling from the sky.

If you hit it off with your honey while flying through the air, he will most likely invite you to join him for the evening's activities. Then the park transforms into a romantic paradise glowing with thousands of twinkling lights. How do I know that these guys woo girls who live large? Most definitely from my courageous girlfriends. You think I have the guts to hop on tremendous roller coasters? Absolutely not! I'm a scaredy-cat to the core. But if you are fearless, by attending Tivoli Park your European love life should instantly intensify.

Word to the Wise. From mid-November to December 30, Tivoli Gardens features a holiday market. Then the amusement park becomes a winter enchantment. All rides still run as Yuletide stalls sell gifts and goodies. I'm sure you can convince your darling Dane to escort you on the 150-year-old, double-decker merry-go-round. On December 24 and 25, Tivoli is closed. Call before your trip to see when the park is open. Hours vary depending on the time of year.

England

England, the birthplace of The Beatles, The Rolling Stones, and Coldplay, is also famous for its art, architecture, and castles. So, what is not so well known that will help you win the hearts of English men?

MAN-MEETING TIDBIT. These guys need time to make an acquaintance. In some other European countries, you could ask a man for directions at a stoplight and he could invite you to the theater. In England, the most you will probably get is a polite answer with a charming accent. These guys are also goal-oriented. When they are going to work or a meeting, that's what's on their minds. If you want their minds on you, use your flirting tips when they are relaxing and being social—in a pub or club, at a park or beach, or enjoying a festival. English men need a solid ten to fifteen minutes to meet you. The following are places where I know women have won their hearts.

London (Leicester Square)

At night on the weekends, Leicester Square, found in the West End district of Central London, is a bustling destination. Since there is always an abundance of man-candy trying to get into the swankiest clubs, the proprietors have representatives roaming the streets searching out alluring girls. If you put on your most flattering outfit, get glamorous, and walk through the Square around 10 or 11 PM, you have a good chance of being approached by one of these attractive male scouts in a sophisticated suit. He will give you a discounted pass to one of the top clubs, and personally escort you through the door and past the long line of Londoners waiting to be admitted.

If you are chosen, you get to choose which club you want to attend. As you are being taken to the door, all the guys standing in line will take notice and consider you a club celeb. Once inside, you will get the star treatment minus the pesky paparazzi (see Tip #9: Dress It Up).

Word to the Fashion Wise. If you wish to be handpicked by a Leicester Square screener, look stunning but avoid slutty. Think Audrey Hepburn, not *Playboy* centerfold. Remember, these are classy clubs. A flowing dress is always a safe bet. Also, wear your hair down. That way, if there is any wind your locks will blow in the breeze as you are strutting through the Square. The goal is to catch the eye of one of the clubs' advance men.

London (Pineapple Dance Studio)

Pineapple is dance studio utopia tucked away on 7 Langley Street, Covent Garden (+44 (0) 20-7836-4004). I strongly suggest that you make this your first London landmark. Pineapple's phenomenal classes will give you the moves to attract the men.

This hot spot was once an old pineapple warehouse. The studio is multileveled. Each room contains mirrors and sprung floors, as well as amazing teachers and dancers. Performers from the theater district practically live there between rehearsing for and appearing in shows. But don't get intimidated. Pineapple is not exclusively for the accomplished. People who have never danced in their lives come to learn the latest club moves.

You also don't have to be an experienced dancer to entice the Brits. Just let the moves from these classes cast their male-catching spells. My friends and I took the combos we learned at Pineapple all throughout Europe. When we used these routines at nightclubs, locals literally circled around us. Pineapple provides classes for all levels, from the beginners to the advanced. The back of the room is the best place to park yourself if you feel at all unsteady, because nobody will notice if you totally mess up. The classes run from morning until night. Visit www.pineapple.uk.com to check out the schedule.

Teachers of the Most Enticing Moves. Although all of the instructors are wonderful, there are two who really teach moves that turn on the men. You will not want to miss out on Xavi's classes. He teaches street dance, performs with entertainers like Dido, Jamelia, Emma Bunton, Gipsy Kings, Blue Peter, and Enrique Iglesias, and choreographs things like Nike promotions. Wow! And once you see his footwork, you will say, "Double wow!" He is so incredible that spectators regularly crowd around his studio window just to get a peek at his fluid dancing precision. When they talk about Xavi's dancing, no matter what language they speak, they use the same three adjectives: "hot, hot, and hot."

Fleur Murray is another hit. She teaches jazz with the three S's: Sass, Sex Appeal, and Seduction. I can't even count the number of times I have used her choreography to grab guys' attention. She is obviously an expert, having appeared in cabarets, music videos, on television, and in the theater. Please don't miss these classes. You know you want to be a showstopper!

Xavi and Fleur can have quite tricky moves even in their so-called easy classes. Don't worry. Nobody cares if you kibosh the combo. It happens all the time.

Caveat. Not all segments of the dances you learn at Pineapple will be appropriate to use at chic clubs. Although you will definitely get your love interest to notice you by sliding on the floor and then extending one leg over your head, you will also probably get kicked out. Pick and choose which moves are best for the hot spot you head out to.

London (The Theater)

If you are into the Artsies—sentimental gents who display their affection by writing you poetry—attending a show is a great opportunity. Read the reviews before you go and know something about the director, actors, and plot. Theater-loving men will be enticed by your knowledge. You will have an edge when striking up a conversation with your romanticist. Hopefully your insights will be so impressive that the man you want to meet will want to continue the discussion in a charming restaurant over drinks.

When I Lured In Olivier the Artsy

I learned how much Artsies are taken in by a girl's theatrical insights while studying European theater in London. We were required to see about twelve plays in two months. We had to read the script and every relevant review before each production and write our own intense analyses afterward. I really do love the theater but it isn't my life's focus, so I would never have gained this much knowledge if it weren't required for the course. Our theater professor really cracked the whip. I later learned that he purposefully gave everyone low grades at the beginning of the course because he was certain that no one could be an excellent critic then. He said we had to breathe in art and have it become part of us to truly understand the theater culture—whatever that means!

Anyway, during the second week we were assigned to see a funky rendition of *Jane Eyre*. At that point, I had two goals. I'd seen a handsome man at the last production that I really wanted to meet, and I was determined to ace the *Jane Eyre* review. I studied like crazy. I didn't even go out on the town for two whole days before the show. When I got to the play—what do you know—I saw the man that I wanted to meet. Well, I reasoned that if he was going to attend two plays in less than a week and a half he was definitely an Artsy. I tried to not get distracted by his emerald green eyes and engaging smile. After all, I had to focus on *Jane Eyre* if I was going to do well in the class. When the final curtain came down I turned to my girlfriend and started fervently brainstorming what I would write about. I analyzed the reviews and even quoted lines from the script. So I might have sounded over the edge to many types of guys, but I wasn't around many types of guys. I was around Artsies.

Emerald Green Eyes, who I soon learned was named Olivier, cut into my conversation, exclaiming, "Excuse me, I don't mean to interrupt, but I completely agree with your viewpoint. You know so much about the theater." Why naturally . . . doesn't everyone?! Conveniently, there was a bar next door with leaded, stained glass windows that looked like they came straight out of Shakespeare's day. It was the perfect post-theater place for an Artsy to take a single girl to get to know her and plan a date. I was afraid that when we were together, Olivier would expect me to have a vast knowledge of plays. Instead, he asked about me. And I didn't need to read the reviews to answer those questions.

From then on, Olivier attended plays that I was assigned to see. If you are going to see a play, why not have an Artsy by your side? After our first liaison a girl in my class said, "That's not fair that you picked up a guy at the theater." Fair? Of course it is! If you put in the effort to study the play, you deserve to pick up the guy. And yes, I got an A in both meeting European men and my theater class.

Romantic Places Artsies Might Take You. I know from Olivier and other Artsies that they get romantic fast. They want to take you to hidden, off-the-beaten-path places like restaurants that have little rooms with drawn curtains for just the two of you. Don't be surprised if your art lover exclaims, accompanied by classical music, "You're more beautiful than Aphrodite, the goddess of beauty and love." Don't think I'm joking. One Artsy told me this followed by, "If you marry me, you will get to enjoy box seats every season for the rest of your life." And he wasn't even drunk when he said this. Wedding rings are overrated when you can just get on with important long-term plans like where to sit at the theater. My girlfriends received equally eloquent devotions from Artsies.

Word to the Theater Wise. If ticket price is a serious issue for you, there are several small London theaters that put on economically priced plays. Many locals hold season tickets, so if you attend more than one London production there is a chance that you will sit near your theatrical target several times! Also, if you are a student, always have your university ID handy. Discounts are often available.

Another Word to the Theater Wise. Another source of cheap theater tickets is TKTS. On the day of the performance, theaters sell their unsold tickets at a steep discount through this venue. If you check out their website at www.tkts.co.uk you can see what tickets are on sale. Then, if you go to one of their booths, located in the Clock Tower building on the south side of the Leicester Square Garden or in the Brent Cross shopping center in Hendon on Prince Charles Drive, you can purchase your half-price tickets.

Oxford
(Market Followed by Punting)

Oxford is known for having great deals at markets. The **Wantage Market**, located in the heart of town, contains not only up-to-the-minute stylish and funky purses, clothes, and knickknacks for next to nothing, but intriguing businessmen who stop through on their lunch breaks. This market is open every Wednesday and Saturday. For the hot European male ticket, stroll through around noon on a Wednesday. Linger at each stall, giving your prospect a chance to comment on the amazing merchandise and excellent prices. Hopefully he'll also be thinking about when you two can meet again. On the last Saturday of each month, there is a farmers' market between 9 AM and 1 PM.

After your new soon-to-be European honey has gotten your number and reluctantly returned to his job, it's time to experience some punting. This involves sitting in a boat that is propelled by a driver maneuvering a large stick as you drift through serene waters and beautiful foliage. At the **Magdalen Bridge Boathouse** (+44 (0) 18-6520-2643), located opposite the Oxford Botanic Garden, you can hire a water chauffeur to take you on a thirty-minute punting tour for about twenty pounds.

There are several perks involved in the punting pleasure. One of the best is watching the guides. Propelling the boat takes a ton of strength, so many of them have amazing bodies. Along with this impressive view, you get to enjoy a magnificent tour and have the chance to ask your knowledgeable water chauffeur about Oxford's exciting events slated for the weekend.

Finland

Finland is beloved for its open spaces, beautiful forests, and icy winters. Its people are known for their hospitality, dancing, and drinking. In the winter when they are outdoors they bundle up, ski, and ice-skate. In the summer, cafés and restaurants spill out onto terraces. All year round, Fins celebrate mini-weekends on Wednesday nights. Ladies not in relationships are sought after in trendy Helsinki, with its equally trendy nightspots. One of the most popular is the luxurious **Lux**, with a collection of five bars and large, inviting terraces. After warming up at Lux, you could cool down at Helsinki's **Arctic Icebar**, a nightclub where you are given gloves as you go through the door. I know, it sounds like such a touristy thing to do, but I have girlfriends who savor that memory. They also savor their man-meeting memories at Lake Kallavesi and on the slopes of Ruka.

Kuopio (Lake Kallavesi)

Kuopio is famous for its ice life. Skating on Lake Kallavesi is Finland's hot—or should I say cold?—pleasure. The ice is open to anyone for several weeks around February and March. Since this site attracts thousands of skaters, you will definitely want to stand out. Finding an adorable snow bunny outfit is just as important as renting your skates. The latter can be accomplished at **Leo's Skate Service** (+358 (0) 40-728-5018) located at the Kuopio Passenger Harbour.

Try gliding in the vicinity of your favorite Fin while calling out an inviting "hei." If gliding is out of your skating league and you are having a hard time just staying on your feet, take heart. Guys love to give advice. Ask your favorite man, or if you are having serious difficulties, the one nearest by, for some guidance. Compliment his skating expertise and you are already in his good graces.

When Miss Newbie Skated into a Fine Fin

Miss Newbie, my friend who met the Austrian guys after Miss Mischievous shoved her down the slope, started a relationship with a dashing Finnish man by what I like to call "falling into his good graces." Skating was new for her. She was making great progress mastering the "stroke," but she had not yet learned the art of the stop when she ran into him. He definitely did not mind. He taught her couples' skating so he could put his arm around her in order to teach her how to stop while keeping her from running into others and protecting her from renegade skaters. At least that is how he explained it to her! This was one of the most charming afternoons of her European trip. When it was over, he invited her to dinner. As you can tell, this girl always had major issues when it came to snow and ice, but not when it came to men. She got all the guys!

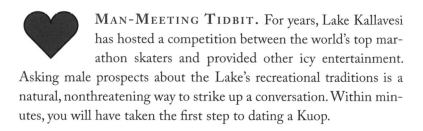

MAN-MEETING TIDBIT. For years, Lake Kallavesi has hosted a competition between the world's top marathon skaters and provided other icy entertainment. Asking male prospects about the Lake's recreational traditions is a natural, nonthreatening way to strike up a conversation. Within minutes, you will have taken the first step to dating a Kuop.

Ruka (The Slopes)

Why indulge in the slopes of Ruka on the southern edge of Lapland? *Pros*: Its stellar snow-blanketed forests, frozen lakes, and starry nights attract the most Finnish foxes—and I don't mean the type that lives in the woods. Ruka has one of the longest skiing and snowboarding seasons, eight months of liveliness starting in October and lasting until May. Travelers on budgets are happy to hear that lift tickets there are known to be sold for some of the lowest prices in Europe. These bargains draw in young people from all over, making Ruka an ideal place to crash for the twenties set. *Cons*: Absolutely none!

Word to the Wise. There are options for those with all levels of slope expertise. If you have never snowboarded, I'd really advise learning. This sport is ultra-popular with the locals. If you are a virgin skier or snowboarder, you have come to the right place. Just log on to www. ruka.fi/winter_eng and sign up for private or group lessons with some of the most experienced slope maneuverers.

MAN-MEETING TIDBIT. Some instructors also have major date potential. So don't waste your lesson, request a male instructor who is single and in your target age range. If you have great chemistry with your fine Fin teacher, maybe he will take you on a mysterious path away from the masses. Rumor has it that Ruka is filled with such routes, so you just need the right native to give you an inside look. Even if your instructor is not a love match, he can give you the lowdown on the singles' scene.

Dining while Meeting Men. When it's time to dine, you can't go wrong on the terrace of **SkiBistro** (+358 (0) 8-860-0300) located in the heart of the action and near Ruka's Bistro Slope. At night, this refuge prides itself on its Finnish rock bands. Party on!

Fashion Flash. Ruka can get enormously cold, like down to twenty degrees below Celsius in the winter. Dress really warm and in layers. Frostbite is not part of your guy-getting European itinerary.

France

France is an excellent location for everything from clubbing to climbing. It has a reputation as the most visited country in the world, with its legendary cosmopolitan cities like Paris, romantic landmarks like the Eiffel Tower, and cultural events like the Cannes Film Festival. For sports enthusiasts, it is also beloved for its beaches, ski resorts, and rural beauty. But if you're planning a French getaway and want to admire the beauty of the European male, visit the venues on the following pages. I have friends who did and were not disappointed.

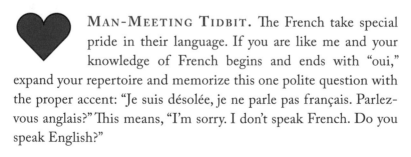 MAN-MEETING TIDBIT. The French take special pride in their language. If you are like me and your knowledge of French begins and ends with "oui," expand your repertoire and memorize this one polite question with the proper accent: "Je suis désolée, je ne parle pas français. Parlez-vous anglais?" This means, "I'm sorry. I don't speak French. Do you speak English?"

In the cities, many Frenchmen, as well as other Europeans, are fluent in English. If you attempt to speak their native tongue, even a little, they will most likely be charmed by your effort and out of courtesy converse freely with you in English. If you do happen to speak the local language, all the better!

Surprising Man-Meeting Asset. All of the girls I know who got French boyfriends did not have large bust lines. When I spoke to Parisians about this phenomenon, they acknowledged that big boobs are generally not a draw for guys from their country. In fact, some consider abundant cleavage to be extra fat and a turnoff. Most of all, they want the girls' bodies to look in proportion. When my girlfriend went to Europe with two curvaceous friends, a group of Frenchmen brushed past them to meet her. Let's just say she is no double D. Men from other European countries were totally speechless when they eyed the vixens by her side. The Sexcapader had ample boobage, which was enviable in most places, but she admitted that France was the hardest spot for her to add stars to her hookup map. So if you are blessed with a voluptuous bust, don't wear a push-up bra or low-cut tops in France. Men from other countries love big boobs, so you can flaunt your assets elsewhere.

Aix-en-Provence (Les Deux Garcons)

If sentimental writers are your cup of tea, then the restaurant Les Deux Garcons located on 53 Cours Mirabeau, 13000 Aix-en-Provence, is a definite destination (+33 (0) 442-260-051). Where else can you fraternize with famous French authors but in this writers' hub? To top off this restaurant's appeal, the men here are known for treating the ladies to drinks, especially to celebrate when their works have been published. You can choose to dine outside while smelling the fresh flowers or inside underneath the ornately painted ceilings. Stay around for the night scene. The upstairs transforms into a *très vogue* piano bar that draws in an eclectic group of musical *hommes*.

Fontainebleau (Rocks)

If you are a rock babe—and I don't mean the music, that's more like London or Amsterdam land—France is the place for you. Hop from rock to rock, from Fontainebleau to Céüse.

Fontainebleau has both a town with a famous Renaissance chateau and a magical hilly forest full of trails, sandstone boulders, and soft, sandy landings. Bouldering here has the quadruple threat: dense sandstone, fantastic friction, intricately shaped stones in a variety of sizes—many with moss—and it is loved by European men. There are climbs for everyone from amateurs to professionals. Some of my girlfriends who are professional climbers say that Fontainebleau gives them a mental, physical, and social workout. They study each boulder before attempting it. Once they embark, it is not unusual for them to be encouraged in a variety of languages by supportive onlookers, and when they reach the top of a difficult boulder, they are often greeted with applause and dancing.

Fontainebleau is also a popular hiking spot. So if you are not up for bouldering, you can still join in the fun, admire the enchanted forest, and meet the European rock-climbing hunks.

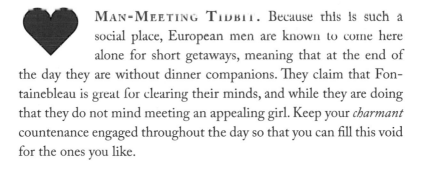 MAN-MEETING TIDBIT. Because this is such a social place, European men are known to come here alone for short getaways, meaning that at the end of the day they are without dinner companions. They claim that Fontainebleau is great for clearing their minds, and while they are doing that they do not mind meeting an appealing girl. Keep your *charmant* countenance engaged throughout the day so that you can fill this void for the ones you like.

Word to the Lodging Wise. There are a variety of reasonably priced places to stay where you can get another chance to meet European men. You can find holiday cottages, called *gîtes*, in the heart of Fontainebleau or in peaceful villages surrounding it. A girlfriend raved about **Maisonbleau**, set on the grounds of a seventeenth-century farmhouse, with accommodations for twelve—her, her girlfriend, and ten new European male acquaintances. Every day while climbing, these girls met people from a variety of countries. They often ran into the same people and built relationships with them, but they said the evenings at the farmhouse were where they really got to know the European men. Campsites are also available. Contact the Fontainebleau tourist office at +33 (0) 160-749-999 or surf Gites-de-France, Gites-Seine-et-Marne, and Camping-de-France websites for options.

Haute Alpes (Céüse/Rocks)

You should never get bored rock climbing in Céüse. I have friends who stayed almost a month and hated to leave. This popular haunt has sensational sectors for varying personalities and skill levels, from **Biographie** with its gigantic overhangs, which appeal to climbers who desire challenge with a dash of danger, to the **Berlin Wall**, which plants the seed of romance with its breathtaking views, and **Un Point Sur L'infini**, which is best for technical gals and attention-to-detail darlings.

Word to the Wise. The best time to visit for a critical mass of European men is from April to August. If you want your accommodations to include European outdoorsmen, stay at **Les Guerins** at 05130 Sigoyer (+33 (0) 492-578-391). This campground is extremely close to the rocks and where most of the climbers crash. In the world of camping, this is the Rolls-Royce of sites. There are hot showers, refrigerators, and washing machines. What more could you ask for? Well, maybe a rockin' hunk. You can also find him here. Some girls have reported that the proprietor of Les Guerins does not speak

English, so if you don't speak French, this is where your pantomiming skills will come in handy. I also hear that the establishment offers dirt-cheap ravioli, so if you are on a tight budget you will never go hungry. And if you are not a big fan of camping in a tent, you can rent a small parked trailer.

Nice (The Beach)

Nice is the home of a beautiful Mediterranean beach where vacationers travel from all over Europe to unwind and have a good time. They bring their towels, bags, and sunscreen and lounge from morning until evening. There is no better place to relax and meet French men.

 MAN-MEETING TIDBIT. The promenade is the prime guy-getting location. This is where your prospects play Frisbee for hours. Take frequent strolls to admire them and let them admire you. In addition to your smashing smile, the most important accessory here is your bathing suit. It better be awfully cute and a style that accentuates your assets. It also wouldn't hurt to amp up those crunches before taking this side trip. The goal here is to land the best beach beau to lead you on a walk through the adorable town and little stores as a prelude to your romantic evening.

Word to the Wise. Instead of sand, this beach is made up of large pebbles. I would advise bringing a yoga mat to tuck under your towel. You won't look your most attractive if you are squirming about uncomfortably . . . but there are always those who defy the odds. Read on!

When the Beach Baby Got Her Glass Filled

I have a friend who strolled along the beach admiring the view, holding an empty glass, and obviously considering places to sit. She was unconcerned that she did not have a mat, or even a towel. A charming gentleman who was admiring his view of her offered to fill her glass and share his beach blanket. This was the beginning of a serious relationship. How serious? Well, let's just say it included wedding bells.

Paris
(O'Sullivans by the Mill and Mandala Ray)

O'Sullivans by the Mill, located at 92 Boulevard de Clichy, is where you will find myriad partiers (+33 (0) 153-090-849). An Irish pub is one of the greatest European male-hunting hot spots in France? You heard me right! At night, O'Sullivans is known for bustling with exciting male hunks. This pub is proud of its dynamite dance parties. Before introductions are even exchanged, guys will encircle you and start dancing. Wear your most appealing dress and use those flirting moves.

 MAN-MEETING TIDBIT. If you can't experience Paris on a Friday or Saturday night, the city's most lively times, then hit up this pub on Thursday night. After all, at O'Sullivans, Thursday is the new Saturday. This is often when the pub features some of the best live bands.

Mandala Ray. If you are in Paris for a weekend visit, I'd suggest planning a celebrity glamour outing the evening after hitting up O'Sullivans. That way you can experience the entire Parisian party spectrum in just two nights. In preparation for living like a movie star, get on that red-carpet cocktail dress and head on over to Mandala Ray, aka Man Ray. With that name I bet you know what you will find. A Paris man indeed! This former movie theater is found on 32-34 Rue Marbeuf, 75008 (+33 (0) 156-883-636). The word on the street is that the ultimate admirers of everything Paris—Johnny Depp, Sean Penn, and John Malkovich—own this restaurant and club. Obviously, you will feel like you are gracing the Oscars as you enter the posh hot spot with its modern décor.

Word to the Wise. Many of the swanky clubs in Paris have a reputation for featuring strict bouncers and steep cover charges. To sidestep these impediments, make a reservation at the restaurant and stay around after dinner for clubbing with the stunning Frenchmen . . . I might add that the restaurant's food is so scrumptious you can visualize Julia Child at the next table relishing it.

When Little Sis Got Caught in a Parisian Love Triangle

Before you head out to the Paris clubs, I want to warn you—this city is very romantic and can easily promote love entanglements. My friend would know. She chose to study there after her big sister in her sorority shared some amazing experiences. Big Sis had met what she thought was her soul mate in a club at the beginning of her semester abroad. He immediately caught her eye with his French John Travolta dancing genes. Their first date was at a charming candlelit restaurant, and they didn't stop dating for the rest of her stay. Everything about Mr. Soul Mate was perfect . . . down to his cooking and the art in his apartment, which happened to be by her favorite painter. When she returned to the States they continued dating long distance. She was sure that one day they would be married.

Well, Little Sis went to Paris hoping to find her own charming French John Travolta. A few days after arriving she met an engaging guy in a club who was a total Groover. They really got along and she confided to him, "My friend is dating a Frenchman who is also an amazing dancer." At the end of the night, he sadly told her that he would like to ask her out, but he had a girlfriend living in another country.

A few days later, Little Sis received a call from her distraught sorority sister, who poured out her sorrow. Mr. Soul Mate had just broken up with her over the phone. Didn't he know they were meant to be together? He told her that even though he loved her, it was just too difficult to date long distance. But she told Little Sis that she had the sneaking suspicion he had met someone else.

That week, Mr. Paris Groover showed up at Little Sis's school declaring that he was no longer in a relationship and would love to take her on a date to a candlelit dinner. What a coincidence! My friend thought, "Candlelit restaurants must be a favorite place for Frenchmen to take girls on first dates."

The following week, Mr. Paris Groover cooked for Little Sis in his apartment. She was stunned to see that he owned the same paintings as the man Big Sis had dated and silently pleaded, "Please tell me all Frenchmen cook and have these paintings in their apartments." Yeah, sure, if the Frenchman's name is Mr. Soul Mate.

After about eight dates, my friend knew without a shadow of a doubt that she was seeing the same guy who had broken up with her sorority sister. The bigger problem was that she knew she was the girl he had dumped Big Sis for. And the even bigger problem was that Little Sis was seriously falling for Mr. Soul Mate.

Are you willing to risk finding yourself in a French love entanglement? If so, then meet the Frenchmen at O'Sullivans by the Mill and Mandala Ray.

Germany

For all you romantics, Germany should be high on the list of places you hope to visit with beautiful castles, palaces, and pastoral country scenes. Germany is also high on the list of places where locals pride themselves on brewing the best beer, throwing fabulous beer festivals, and cultivating congenial beer gardens. Of course, it has the winning European combination of clubbing, pubbing, hiking, biking, skiing, and snowboarding. With this variety of adventures awaiting you, all forty flirty tips can be put to good use . . . and did I mention that German men love beer?

MAN-MEETING TIDBIT. In this country the people are known for saying exactly what they think. They are not trying to be mean; they just believe that complete honesty is the best policy. One of my friends was told sincerely by a German man who had not known her long, "You are the total love of my life." And he meant it. Another was told that she needed to get her hair cut.

When Mr. Direct Helped
Miss Savvy Businesswoman Home

Actually, the German gents do not have to know you at all to dispense their personal insights. Once, during a European festival when the cab companies unexpectedly quit dispatching, my girlfriend asked a German guy for help determining the right bus to take back to her hotel. She knew her address, but did not have directions since she had taken a cab to her destination and planned to take a cab back. The German man did help her, but first he observed, "That was not smart of you to not have directions back to your hotel. You're a naïve traveler." Don't beat around the bush now . . . just say what you really think! As my friend talked further with him, she realized that he really did care. He was concerned that she would go out again without her directions, get lost, and not be able to find help. My girlfriend was actually a savvy businesswoman. She learned from this German man to be a savvy direction woman too.

Berlin (Kastanienallee)

Kastanienallee is a Berlin road bustling with locals at restaurants, bars, and fashion shops. Half of it is located in the neighborhood of Prenzlauer Berg and the other half in Mitte. During the day, you can find all types of Germans, from singles to families to grandparents who have lived to see the Berlin Wall go up and come down. But at night this is the young European singles' haunt. For the men, the most sought-after attraction is the **Prater Beer Garden** located on Kastanienallee 7-9, Prenzlauer Berg, 10435 (+49 (0) 30-448-5688).

A beer garden is basically what it sounds like—Europeans enjoying beer in a garden on picnic benches, often while watching sports on large screens. Prater, founded in 1837, is the oldest beer garden in the country and has always been a man magnet. I have heard countless guys talk about how this place is the "best ever." Well, the European men love it so much that they often outnumber the girls five to one . . . And this place is ginormous with six hundred seats. So you could have five hundred European men to choose from. No complaining here!

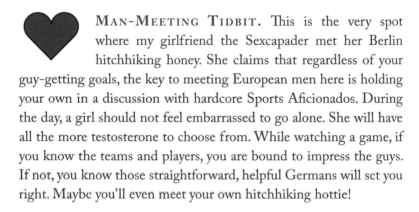 MAN-MEETING TIDBIT. This is the very spot where my girlfriend the Sexcapader met her Berlin hitchhiking honey. She claims that regardless of your guy-getting goals, the key to meeting European men here is holding your own in a discussion with hardcore Sports Aficionados. During the day, a girl should not feel embarrassed to go alone. She will have all the more testosterone to choose from. While watching a game, if you know the teams and players, you are bound to impress the guys. If not, you know those straightforward, helpful Germans will set you right. Maybe you'll even meet your own hitchhiking hottie!

Word to the Wise. Prater Beer Garden is open every day from April through September starting at noon, as long as the weather permits. They only take cash, so stash up and enjoy.

Berlin (Oranienburger Straße)

Oranienburger Straße is located in the neighborhood of Mitte right next to Kastanienallee. It is a little over a mile long and filled with man-meeting bars, cafés, and restaurants with an abundance of—I bet you know what—beer! This area is known for attracting travelers, but don't be deterred, because many are Europeans on weekend trips. There is not one single haunt that sticks out for feel or décor, but most are filled with male prospects, especially on Friday and Saturday nights. Peer in and see which one fits your fancy.

When Miss Alluring Got a Bottomless Bar Tab

Since Oranienburger Straße is big on attracting travelers, if you go several times, you will probably not keep seeing the same faces . . . that is, except for the bartenders, who can be hard to forget. One of my friends—let's call her Miss Alluring—studied in Berlin for a semester. Several nights a week, she stopped in at a bar in Oranienburger Straße for a study break. One particular spot had an especially appealing bartender. As Miss Alluring became a regular, she noticed a trend. Whenever she ordered a drink from this bartender, he gave her the bill with zero amount due. And I heard the economy was affecting people's budgets . . . apparently not my girlfriend's. Each time, she showed him the bill and said that there must be a mistake, but the bartender assured her that there was none. The message was always delivered with his killer smile. Well, this went on for a few weeks. Then the bartender gave Miss Alluring her zero bar tab with his phone number written on it. What did he want in return? A date!

Munich (Oktoberfest)

Oktoberfest should really be renamed Manfest. When the fall leaves turn, this is where guys head. Beers here are brewed darker and stronger especially for Oktoberfest. Everyone says that this is absolutely the best place for beer drinking. How could it not be? The beer here is enjoyed in highly festive lodge-style tents packed with European men in party mode and filled with the music of traditional German bands.

About six million people attend the sixteen- to eighteen-day festival, which starts around the third week of September depending on the year. Six million festivalgoers means you have a whole ton of *männer* to choose from!

MAN-MEETING TIDBIT. Each tent at Oktoberfest is sponsored by a different beer company. If you hope to get admitted into one, come early—at least by 11 AM. Each tent holds only so many partiers and fills up quickly. After that, admittance is strictly one-in one-out and patrons park in those tents for hours, so you may never get in.

If that happens, don't despair. This can be a blessing in disguise. All the rejects commiserate on a wooden-planked deck outside each tent while waiting for an opening. Since beer is also served out there, this is a very social environment. German gents will want you to join them in a toast to your mutual misfortune at missing out on admittance. If you like beer, you could be in for several free drinks. If you don't, sip up the good company. After bonding with the friendly foreigners, you will be glad that you were relegated to the terrace.

Word to the Wise. To see this year's schedule check out www .oktoberfest.de/en.

Greece

For single girls seeking Greek gods, this is your place! Greek men give a new meaning to the word "gorgeous." You can meet them everywhere from Piraeus, the charming boating gateway to the Saronic Islands, to Athens, the liveliest city in the country.

MAN-MEETING TIDBIT. According to my friends who have dated them, Greek men are all about chivalry and love of family. In fact, because of the emphasis on family, they tend to treat their wives and mothers phenomenally well, meaning that single Greek men will probably treat you the same way.

In addition to their families, the Greeks are all about festivals. There are national festivals honoring Greek history; cultural festivals filled with music, theater, and the arts; and religious festivals based on the Greek Orthodox calendar. This country has so many festivals that you can find one almost any month that you choose to visit.

My Greece-going girlfriends said that single Greek gods are especially at home in Kolonaki—the epicenter of Athens—Crete's rugged hillsides, and the beach life and nightlife of Mykonos. They each found their Adonis in one of the following hot spots.

Athens (Kolonaki)

This neighborhood is the chic center of Greece. It is an older, posh district full of boutiques, coffee houses, restaurants, and galleries. Ultra-upscale equals a very expensive place to live. Translation: There are lots of established men who thrive in this environment and would enjoy showing you all that Kolonaki has to offer.

Stroll through the area next to the scenic hills and stop in at any of the coffee shops. Take off your coat and stay awhile—this is where the Greek celebrities take breaks. Make eye contact and lure in those businessmen bombshells. Hopefully one will invest in you. While dining with your Greek idol, you may even get a glimpse of the Saronic Islands.

When Miss Calm Tamed the Intense Aristotle

Obviously Kolonaki is known for attracting the About Business prospects, but the Greeks in this category have their own unique, lovable qualities. My girlfriend who dated one wanted me to let the single girls know that About Business Greek men are extremely charming and thoughtful, but very intense in every aspect of their lives, from building careers to pursuing women. As a result, they are especially drawn to calm females who balance them out. My friend fits that description perfectly. Miss Calm dated an About Business Greek man named Aristotle . . . for real! He was a medical student preparing to become a surgeon and she said that Webster should really add his name under the definitions for the words "intense" and "flawless," because like many Greek guys, this About Business was beyond attractive.

To describe Aristotle's personality, I want to tell you the story of when he first started dating Miss Calm. He asked her if she wanted to go on a bike ride before their first class of the day. Miss Calm visualized a romantic biking trail next to a river . . . maybe stopping for breakfast along the way. Apparently she didn't know Aristotle well enough yet. When he showed up wearing spandex, she knew this was no leisurely biking date. Aristotle did want to get to know Miss Calm, but he also wanted to get in ample exercise so that his endorphins would sustain him during his rigorous neuroscience classes. The trail was not along a river. Instead, there were lots of hills. Aristotle cycled so quickly that Miss Calm could not keep up. He would bike a ways out and then loop back around to see Miss Calm. This pattern repeated itself several times as my friend's muscles started burning so badly that she wondered if instead of attending class that day she would have to schedule an emergency massage.

If you find yourself in a similar situation, just kindly explain to your Greek man how you feel. Miss Calm says that from dating Aristotle she learned that these men want to make women happy, but they are so programmed to go with gusto that they often don't realize how hard this can be on others. Her solution was to let Aristotle get his endorphins by himself in the morning and then go for a romantic ride with her in the evening when the work was done and he could focus on his sweetheart. Once Miss Calm learned how to handle her stunning About Business Grecian, their relationship was rolling.

Another friend of mine, Miss Mellow, also dated an About Business Greek man and found an asset in his intensity. She helped him stay calm in tense situations and he helped her ratchet up her concentration when it was necessary.

 MAN-MEETING TIDBIT. Traditional Greeks are known for waking up early and heading off to work without eating breakfast. By about 9 or 10 AM, they usually stop for a pastry snack at one of the nearby cafés. Then, around noon or 1 PM, it is lunchtime. Dinner comes at about 9 PM. Make sure to plan your café and restaurant trips accordingly so that you get to eat with the locals, not when there is a lull. Also, don't cruise the town between 2 and 4 PM. The natives will be in bed enjoying their siestas. I'd advise you to do the same. Grecians stay up until at least 1 or 2 AM every night.

Mykonos (Beaches and Nightlife)

This town is packed with stylish beaches, bars, restaurants, and shops. It has developed a glamorous reputation without losing its Greek roots. During the summer, girls live in their bikinis all day until evening. Even if they decide to take a hike, head out to a restaurant, or shop, they often simply throw on a sarong and go.

When the weather is good and the sun begins to set, jump over to **Tropicana**, located on Paradise Beach, 84600, Mykonos, Cyclades Islands (+30 2289-023-582). Here almost everyone will still be in swimming suits and cover-ups for a buzzing beach party. Actually, this hot spot is open all day for food, so you can start your morning there and end it with a beach party that lasts through the "early evening," which is considered to be from seven to well past ten.

The "real evening" begins around 11 PM. Then the party-going masses change out of their swimsuits and move to the bars and clubs. When the weather is hot, the bars and clubs set up shop at the beach. The night ends at daybreak.

One of the best nighttime destinations is **Skandinavian Bar and Disco**, located on Ag. Ioannis Barkia (+30 2289-022-669). Single girls consider it a popular place to rendezvous with European men they met at the beach during the day. The haunt is known by the natives as "Skandi," so if you want to fit in with the Greek men, call it by that nickname. This jamming hot spot takes up an entire block and is teeming with European men wanting to meet single girls.

Holland –
The Netherlands

The Netherlands is commonly referred to as Holland, but this is actually incorrect. North and South Holland are only two of the twelve provinces in the country. So if you want to make a good first impression on the native males, it would be a good idea to know that

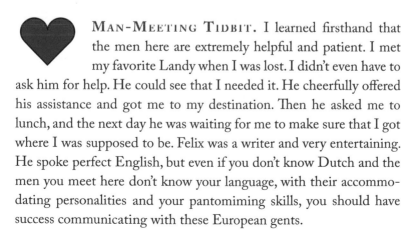

MAN-MEETING TIDBIT. I learned firsthand that the men here are extremely helpful and patient. I met my favorite Landy when I was lost. I didn't even have to ask him for help. He could see that I needed it. He cheerfully offered his assistance and got me to my destination. Then he asked me to lunch, and the next day he was waiting for me to make sure that I got where I was supposed to be. Felix was a writer and very entertaining. He spoke perfect English, but even if you don't know Dutch and the men you meet here don't know your language, with their accommodating personalities and your pantomiming skills, you should have success communicating with these European gents.

In the summer, the big draw in the Netherlands is the international language of music. There are outdoor festivals featuring concerts in everything from pop to classical to almost ancient. The **Lowlands Festival**, in August, is specially designed for bonding with the natives (www.lowlands.nl/english.php). I have also heard of close encounters between single girls and Landies at Paradiso in Amsterdam and Scheveningen in The Hague.

Amsterdam (Paradiso)

Paradiso is Amsterdam's pop temple. If you're turned on by Rock Stars, roll on over to Weteringschans 6 (+31 (0) 20-626-4521). This old church was converted into a hippie hangout during the late sixties. Now Paradiso hosts some of the world's most famous artists and draws in the craziest crowds. Just to etch the surface, this legendary hot spot has housed the Velvet Underground, Macy Gray, Justin Timberlake, Lenny Kravitz, the Rolling Stones, Nirvana, Prince, and Beck. While you're jamming to the musical stars' greatest hits, the original gorgeous stained-glass windows of the church will be vibrating to the bass. Is that not totally awesome? To scout out concert ticket prices see www.paradiso.nl.

Fashion Flash. Amsterdam has an atmosphere where anything goes. Although wearing your lacy dress on a fancy date to one of Kolonaki's posh restaurants is optimum, this will not fly in Paradiso's pop culture. If you are ultra-feminine and love frills, get appropriately rockified before stepping foot in this nightclub.

The Hague (Scheveningen)

Scheveningen has the sexiest beach in the Netherlands, bar none. In the summer, you can find more Landies and other Europeans males here than the Lowlands Festival has bands (but don't get me wrong, those bands have a mega-load of men in them too). During the day, this beach is known for having fabulous water sports and stunning European male surfers and kiteboarders. I learned just the trick for meeting them from a male surfer himself. He said that these athletes love their sports and get extremely immersed in them, so just looking cute won't usually pull them away from their boards to meet you. Instead you will have to **SURF**. This is not the kind of surfing that any ordinary instructor can teach you. It goes as follows:

<u>S</u>unscreen. Just put sunscreen on your face before heading to the beach. When you arrive, position yourself in front of the surfers and boarders, take off your top, and apply lotion to your body while posing appealingly but naturally. By telling you to take off your shirt, I'm not advocating that you start a topless community. I just mean take off the cover-up over your bikini top.

I know what some of you girls are probably thinking: "I shouldn't have to pose to attract men." Or, "I would feel ridiculously silly posing." The latter was my exact response, but my surfing friend assured me that I should try it. So I did and, trust me, it works—but only if you act . . .

<u>U</u>naware that you are trying to attract guys, otherwise you can come off as self-conscious. No matter how charming you are, self-conscious girls won't lure in these athletes. The first time I tried this tip, I felt so ill at ease that I attracted odd stares instead of studs. The goal in the SU part of SURF is to get the water hotties to be drawn to you. Then they will be more likely to want to help when you . . .

<u>R</u>ide. Get on the board and try it. Once you reach the SUR in SURF, the chances are that the men will want to help you,

and helping you is the first step in dating you. Another tactic is to . . .

Find a cute surfing instructor and sign up for lessons. European athletes often travel around from country to country following the sun and teaching water sports.

When Blondie de Femme Mastered the SURF

I have this girlfriend, let's call her Blondie de Femme because she has light blonde hair, a gorgeous little figure, and ultra-feminine charm. Once, when she was on a one-week vacation to a beach similar to Scheveningen, she took a lesson from an Italian instructor named Constantin Scandiano. So this guy won't be Google-imaged and gazed at, I altered his name . . . but the real one does contain, I kid you not, the words "scan" and "tan." My friend wanted to do more than just *scan* this *tan* site. I saw a picture of the guy and he was seriously sizzling . . . an Air Brushed all the way. I thought twelve-packs only came in beer. Well, I was wrong. They come in Constantin's abs!

Blondie de Femme was so distracted by Scandiano's good looks, fun personality, and the fact that he kept paying her special attention that she fell off her board. OK, so she's not going to be a professional surfer, but what girl wouldn't fall off her board when an Air Brushed jokingly tells her he loves her? Maybe in Constantin's case it wasn't a joke. He abandoned his board to be with her out of the ocean while she was in town. They spent several evenings together and she got to do way more than just scan his tan.

She was delighted to learn that Italians know how to dress. Most men think there are two types of underwear: boxers and briefs. To Italians, there is only one—Dolce & Gabbana. And you wondered why single girls love Italian guys . . . I hereby rest my case!

My friend is now a senior in college planning to attend graduate school in Europe. She and Constantin are still in touch and she expects to have many more unofficial boarding lessons and official dates with him in Italy.

Back to Scheveningen—after you finish SURFing the day away, bounce down the boardwalk. There are lots of bars and restaurants where the water cuties and other Europeans unwind.

Hungary

Hungarian men have a reputation for being dashing, intelligent, and entrepreneurial. Every year since the Soviet Union first began to release its grip on the country, this has proven true. Hungary has become one of the most vibrant places in the world and their male-meeting meccas, which I am about to reveal, are among the most creative. Hungarians are privately very proud of these accomplishments, but it is not within their national character to brag about them. Recently, I was talking with an attractive twenty-seven-year-old Hungarian man who was in Los Angeles on business. I related the wonders I had heard of the club A38. He was deeply touched and explained how hard the Hungarian people have worked to develop Budapest and the effort that went into A38. So if you want to find a way into a Hungarian man's heart, genuinely compliment his country. It's easy to do!

MAN-MEETING TIDBIT. Girlfriends who have visited Hungary tell me that the native men pride themselves on being courteous. They are particularly patient with those who do not know their language. This is one of those countries where men will be charmed by any of your attempts to learn anything in their native tongue and patiently help you. Mr. International Businessman confirms this assessment. He does a lot of deals with Hungarians and says that the men are also honest and family-oriented. Since his daughter just got married, he particularly values these traits. He believes that Hungarian men make good husbands. If a single girl wants to get into a serious relationship with one of them, he wholeheartedly supports it.

Budapest (A38)

Ahoy girlies! A38, originally a Ukrainian stone-carrier ship built in—you guessed it—1938, was hauled all the way from the Ukraine to Budapest. There it underwent major reconstruction and was set afloat in the Danube. April 30, 2003, marked the opening of this hot hub found on Petofi Bridge in the Buda side of Budapest (for program information: +36 (06) 1-464-3940; for restaurant: +36 (06) 1-464-3946). Wanna become a sea goddess? Then book your Budapest trip for an A38 tête-à-tête. Go to www.a38.hu/?l=_en to see the list of events.

There are enclaves on board for all personality types. A38 is where noteworthy musicians hold concerts, directors stage plays, and wine connoisseurs toast guests. This ship's club is known for attracting lust-worthy Hungarians, so dance as long as it takes to meet your seductive sea mate. Then grab some fresh air on the roof terrace.

Are you hungry? If not, just say the country's name and you will be craving the delicious food served in the A38 restaurant . . . not to mention the accommodating waiters serving you by gigantic windows that show off stunning river and city views. What more of a dazzling evening could you desire? The restaurant is in such high demand that your *férfi* might have to make a reservation for the following evening, but waiting isn't a bad alternative. That gives you more time to hang with your Hungary honey. You'd better be game! This is Budapest's beloved vessel.

Budapest (Ship Factory Island)

Nicknamed "Dream Island" and referred to as Hajógyári Sziget by the locals, this party paradise was once a ship factory. The island is in the middle of the Danube and houses several beach clubs that attract thousands of natives and travelers from other European countries. Feel free to flip between these eclectically themed gatherings. Dress to impress. Here Budapest bouncers pride themselves on booting out the scrubs. Scruffy is not the new sexy.

Three of the top clubs where you should be guaranteed to get charming European men are **White Angel** (+36 (06) 30-691-3000), **Dokkoló** (+36 (06) 30-455-0400), and **Dokk** (+36 (06) 30-535-2747). You might be tempted to take a nap at the White Angel among the curtains and candles, but prop open those eyes. The company there is way too charismatic. During the summer the owner of White Angel opens another club on the sand about a mile away, called **Bed Beach** (+36 (06) 30-436-4400).

Dokkoló is known as the most social ship, and Dokk wins the award for gorgeous guys with their gorgeous sports cars parked at the entrance. Like White Angel, from mid-May to mid-September, Dokk opens a beach club about two hundred meters away at **Dokk Beach**. It has a bridge leading to a platform on the water where club-goers can find romance under the stars at night.

Iceland

Iceland . . . just saying the name might make you think *burrrrrrr!* Actually, this stunning region, with its amazing icecaps, glaciers, spraying geysers, rambunctious rivers, and waterfalls, is not that cold. In fact, in the cities on an average winter day, the temperature is about the same as in New York. You can visit summer and winter and have an equally mantastic trip.

So why exactly is this country called Iceland if it's not that cold? Well, there is a legend that the first Viking to set foot on the beautiful island wanted to keep it all to himself so he named it "Iceland" to fool everyone into thinking that the whole place was made of ice. Like that was going to work! People learned that Iceland was a place not to stay away from. Even though the area became inhabited, it is still one of the least populated countries, with only a little over 300,000 citizens, and is generally considered one of the best bargain vacation spots.

A popular novelty of this area is that people swim in geothermally heated outdoor pools, even during blizzards. My friend went on a date with a European man that involved dinner and a dip in one of these pools. Most girls consider kissing in the pouring rain to be romantic, like the iconic scene in *The Notebook*. Imagine kissing in a blizzard while staying cozily warm. That's like romantic to the tenth degree!

So, if you like an intimate and friendly feel with an emphasis on outdoor sports, you will want to visit Iceland. You will also want to become intimate with the chiseled mountain guides. What type of men are these? Obviously Airbrushed Outdoor Sports Aficionados!

Fagurholsmyri (Skaftafell National Park)

Hiking in Skaftafell National Park is a total treat. It is located at 785 Öraefi (+354 470-8300 for information, guided tours; skaftafell@ ust.is). The breathtaking landscape is set between sand and glacier, with a visually diverse scene including the glacier cap, rock, water, and wildlife. The area is known for its magnificent bird-watching and, of course, man-watching. For you geology babes, one of the beauties of this place is the occasional instance when, under the Vatnajökull ice cap, the intense heat from one of the greatest geothermal sites contrasts with the cold from Europe's largest glacier to bring fire and ice together. OK, for you girls who think of geology as rocks for jocks— and since you clearly aren't a jock, you're a hiking goddess—you may want me to get on to describing how to meet the Icelandic men and enjoy the scenic landscapes without thinking about what is going on under your feet. This is just the place.

Word to the Hiking Wise. If you do travel alone, having a tour guide is not only safe but gives you a total in with the locals. Tour guides themselves are often European dating possibilities who can show you around. Many of these men work as guides to keep themselves in shape for doing other physical jobs like stunt work in movies. So if you hunger for hot bods, sign up to see the natural sights with one of them. There are many tour guides in Europe. Choose one who works for a reputable company. That way the company will be checking in on him and he will want to take extra special care to keep you safe and show you a wonderful time. Several friends have suggested the **Icelandic Mountain Guides**. See www.mountainguides.is for the options.

When the Blond Adonis Guided Hiking Hottie

I know a sporty girl, Hiking Hottie, who had time off from work and wanted to travel to Iceland and journey through Skaftafell National Park. Sadly, none of her friends had breaks at the same time so she was left companionless. She didn't let this stop her. She signed up for a guided tour through Icelandic Mountain Guides.

When Hiking Hottie arrived at the National Park on a beautiful summer evening, she unrolled her sleeping bag and got excited to meet her guide the next morning. Noticing that she did not have a tent, some other male guides—who I might reemphasize were gorgeous—said she shouldn't sleep out in the elements. They offered to let her stay in the guides' tent. Reality flash: These guys weren't saying this like, "Hey Hiking Hottie, wanna sleep in our tent? Wink wink!" They were being protective. During the night, another guide checked in on them. Noticing the random body, he flashed his light on Hiking Hottie. She opened her eyes to see a six-foot blond Adonis looking back in bewilderment. She quickly explained the situation, he apologized, and she went back to sleep.

The next morning Hiking Hottie met her tour guide—the blond Adonis from the night before. Except on their second meeting she got to see him after brushing her teeth, having her hair ready for adequate flipage, and changing into her cute hiking outfit . . . not to mention without being abruptly awakened with a flashlight shining in her eyes. They got along great. Not only did he have an amazing body, he had brains. The landscapes were even more enthralling to see when accompanied by his fun commentary.

When Hiking Hottie's Friend Found True Love

The blond Adonis became more than a guide, and Hiking Hottie had such a fabulous Iceland experience that she urged her girlfriend to visit Skaftafell National Park on her next vacation and hire a guide too. This tip worked so well for her friend that she and her guide fell in love. They dated long distance for four years, visiting each other as much as possible. Then they realized how rare it would be to find another companion as compatible. Now they are happily married. They spend half of the year at their US home and half in Iceland. They lead tours together as often as possible and always make time for romantic hikes in remembrance of that first trip to the National Park where fire and ice came together and so did their hearts. They just celebrated the birth of their first child.

Word to the Camping Wise. If you want to go camping anywhere in Iceland, check out www.gocamping.is. It provides the latest details about the various campsites.

Ireland

This beautiful emerald island is surrounded by hundreds of isles and inlets and shared by two countries. The Republic of Ireland covers five-sixths of it, and Northern Ireland, which is part of the United Kingdom, takes up the rest. This split, which happened in the 1920s, was not amicable, and Northern Ireland gained a reputation as a dangerous place, but conditions have substantially improved in recent years as the movement to bring Ireland together has gained momentum.

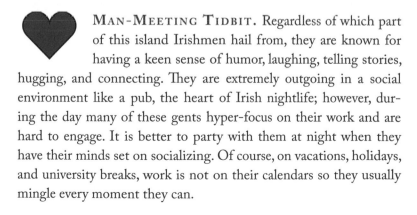 **MAN-MEETING TIDBIT.** Regardless of which part of this island Irishmen hail from, they are known for having a keen sense of humor, laughing, telling stories, hugging, and connecting. They are extremely outgoing in a social environment like a pub, the heart of Irish nightlife; however, during the day many of these gents hyper-focus on their work and are hard to engage. It is better to party with them at night when they have their minds set on socializing. Of course, on vacations, holidays, and university breaks, work is not on their calendars so they usually mingle every moment they can.

Fashion Flash. In the singles' circles, Irish girls always try to attract the local lads by dressing to the nines and wearing high heels, short skirts, and intense makeup. The practice is so widespread that if you do not adopt this uniform, Irish guys may think you will not welcome their advances. Two of my friends experienced this firsthand. They were dining at a café one wintry evening wearing jeans, sweaters, and scarves. Two attractive Irish gents told them that they noticed the absence of a ring on their left hands and wondered if they were dressed that way to give off the message that they were not interested in meeting "handsome, charming Irishmen" such as themselves. Surprised, my friends responded that they were just trying to stay warm.

Dublin (St. Patrick's Festival)

Obviously there is no better place to celebrate St. Patty's Day than with the Irish! In Dublin, this holiday isn't just honored on March 17; it encompasses about six days of festivities showcasing some of the best Irish talent and attended by some of the best Irishmen. Since the festival is charmed by leprechaun luck, if you go you should be lucky enough to snatch one.

The history of this holiday began with a teenage boy, Maewyn Succat from the fifth century, who was kidnapped and forced into slavery. After six years, he escaped and had a vision to help the Irish people. He took the vows of a priest, changed his name to Patrick, and dedicated his life to following his vision. Today, in the spirit of honoring this saint, over 600,000 people attend Dublin's St. Patrick's Festival. If you go, be prepared for more than one twenty-first-century Irish hunk to change his name to "St. Lover" and try to sweep you off your feet. Wear green, hold that four-leaf clover close, set your eyes on your favorite Irish lad, and get ready to laugh at his jokes and take pleasure in his romantic pursuits while joining in the festivities.

Word to the Wise. There are also many events to enjoy in the days leading up to the festival. Check out www.stpatricksfestival.ie/cms/events.html for the details. Some shindigs attract kids, some families, some older couples, and other singles . . . so choose events that interest both you and eligible Irishmen.

Dublin (Temple Bar)

Temple Bar, Dublin's cultural center, has preserved its medieval, narrow, cobblestoned streets for a lovely ambiance. It is a wonderful location to take a daytime stroll, a great dining destination with its many restaurants, and the ideal place for a nighttime jaunt . . . or should I say dance? After the sun sets, there are often street performers and people dancing on the sidewalks. To sum it up, Temple Bar has it all.

One of the district's best pubs is called **The Temple Bar Pub**—I know, such a creative name. It can be found at 48 Temple Bar (+353 (0) 1-672-5287). But seriously, check it out! This multi-storied haunt is like, "Calling all Irishmen." It is also eye-catching, with its bright red walls, authentic Irish décor, and beer garden out back. The interior has stacks of bottles that reach to the ceiling. You know you are in Ireland the instant you enter.

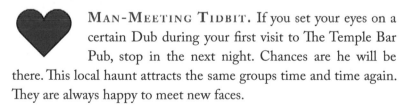

MAN-MEETING TIDBIT. If you set your eyes on a certain Dub during your first visit to The Temple Bar Pub, stop in the next night. Chances are he will be there. This local haunt attracts the same groups time and time again. They are always happy to meet new faces.

Other Mantastic Areas of Temple Bar. Some pubs in Temple Bar are considered "touristy" by the locals—"touristy" meaning attracting a ton of European travelers, especially the English, French, and Scots.

Lots of my girlfriends have wholeheartedly suggested this center for meeting European men. They say that if you hear a demeaning comment about this zone, delete it from your memory.

When the Sexcapader Enticed the Irish Firemen

You can meet European males practically anywhere in Temple Bar. The Sexcapader and some girlfriends even met some entertaining Irish firemen at a stoplight. This girl really knows how to use what she's got. She posed so that the guys could admire her voluptuous figure—unlike the French, Irishmen wholeheartedly embrace girls with ample bust lines—then she asked the firefighters, "Hey, can we come to the station and take some pictures of your fire truck?" So that's what they call it these days in Ireland! Well, the guys caught on to her code words and replied, "We'd love to entertain you." Part of the festivities involved taking pictures of the girls sliding down the fire poles accompanied by pulsating Irish music. This was "Girls Gone Wild Irish Style."

The party was cut short when the guys received an emergency call. Well, I don't know if most people would consider 6 AM cut short! The girls got to ride home in the fire truck and were given Irish fire-fighting shirts as keepsakes. The Sexcapader still wears hers— that is, while admiring her star map of liaisons with European men.

Obviously, this man-meeting story comes from the crazy end of the single girl spectrum, but I have it on good authority that any type of girl can find her match at Temple Bar.

Galway (The Square and Shop Street)

Galway is a total college town. About half of the students attending the National University of Ireland are Irish. The rest come from a variety of nations. This area is small enough to have an intimate, friendly feel, but the residents know how to party just as well as those in the big cities. The Square and Shop Street are the highlights of the social scene day and night.

Word to the Wise. Communicating with locals about The Square can be a little confusing because it goes by three names, and that is probably why they mostly just call it "The Square." In 1710 when this luscious green park in the center of the city was created, it was called Eyre Square, after the mayor. In 1965, it was officially renamed Kennedy Memorial Park in honor of President John F. Kennedy, one of Ireland's favorite famous sons, who visited Galway just before his assassination. The love Galway shows in honoring him is transferred to the love Irishmen show toward single girls in this park. The Square is surrounded by streets that link it to Shop Street, a car-free zone with cobblestones, beautiful brick buildings, pubs, street performers, and the best shopping in the city.

The Single Girl's Dream Galway Itinerary

Day Life in Galway

Grab some breakfast and lounge in The Square when the sun is high in the sky. My girlfriend who has had great man-meeting success here suggests planning a trip during a short university break. You can call the school to find out when these breaks are held any given year (+353 (0) 91-524-411). Unlike many universities, in Galway when students are out of school for a short time they generally stay in town, put their books away, and set their schedules for mingling. My friend visited during a winter break and found The Square swarming with Irish students eager to make new friends and touch base with old ones.

Fashion Flash for the Warm and Trendy. My Galway-loving girl-friend is from the southern US, so Ireland seemed incredibly freezing to her at that time of year. She was amazed to see that even during the frigid winter, Irish girls were scantily dressed to impress . . . but then you could have guessed that from your Irish Fashion Flash. My girl-friend felt isolated all bundled up in her under armor, thick sweater, down jacket, and multiple scarves while the Irish ladies were brav-ing the elements in their usual attire—miniskirts and heels. Since for them this is de rigueur, maybe their bodies have adjusted to the cold. If you do not have the constitution to wear the "Irish guy-getting uniform" in cold weather but want to join in the spirit of it, I'd suggest investing in a little thermal jacket and mittens with hand warmers to compensate for your minimal clothing on the lower shanks. You could also get disappearing nylons or trendy beige fishnets. Then you would have the bare-legged look minus the goose bumps. It's hard to pick up an Irish lad when your teeth are chattering. Sipping hot chocolate outdoors is also a good warming tactic. My friend got hooked on it as well as the Irishmen.

Nightlife in Galway

Shop Street is filled with guy-getting pubs. After you relax at the park during the day, head over there, hit up the shops, and slide into a pub. One of my girlfriends—let's call her Miss Masters because she is getting her masters at the National University of Ireland—says this is where the eligible college guys unwind. Being very astute and meticulously organized, Miss Masters mapped out the best times and places to meet the men. Here is how she says you can capitalize on the Irish male goods any night of the week.

9 to 11 PM. Grab a drink at a bar or pub. Or better yet, visit a number of pubs in Shop Street and around Galway. Once you have befriended some desirable European men, on some nights instead of hitting up the bars you can plan pre-gaming parties from 10 to 11

PM. Teach the Irishmen the drinking game Kings. Hardly anyone from Ireland knows this game and they instantly *love* it. But only play for about an hour, because if you go much longer you will definitely not top it off at tipsy. Then you won't be able to walk to the clubs. Plus, once you start slurring your words, the Irishmen will no longer be impressed.

Kings is a great, nonthreatening way to get to know the Irish guys better. If you don't drink alcohol, you can still participate. In college, I played all the drinking games with cranberry juice. I know . . . I'm a hard hitter! I hear that pure cranberry juice is good for your skin. So for the nondrinkers, while you are meeting the Irishmen you will be giving your skin a beauty treatment. If you are really strict about your health and beauty regimen, you will want to switch to water halfway through the game.

Go to www.kingskup.com to purchase your waterproof cards for Kings. Every card contains the rules of the game.

11 to Closing (About 2 or 3 AM). Hit the clubs. Here are Miss Masters' three favorites: First, **Cuba**, located on 11 Prospect Hill, Galway, 1 (+353 (0) 91-565-991). This club usually features techno, alternative rock, or pop music. Unless you arrive by 11 PM, the line to get inside can become enormously long. You can sidestep that by coming earlier and enjoying **Bar 903** downstairs.

Second, **GPO**, found on 21 Eglinton St. (+353 (0) 91-563-073). This club is all about fun, with its bright lights and guy-getting atmosphere. It is great on any night of the week, but on Monday nights it is usually known as the "*biggest* student party" in town. As the Irish would say, "how bad!"

Third, **Karma**, located at 28 Eyre Square (+353 (0) 91-500-330). This hopping night spot is right off The Square and tied into the **Skeffington Arms** hotel, which is known for creating special packages that pamper single girls. I realize the address can be a bit confusing because of The Square's name change to Kennedy Memorial

Park. If you think of Kennedy Park as being within The Square, aka Eyre Square, you won't go wrong. Karma is at the heart of Irish nightlife and hosts amazing theme parties. Check out the events before you go at www.karma.ie/index1.htm and be prepared to get decked out to match the theme.

To peruse the Skeffington Arms hotel's girl-power packages—like "Sex & the City," "Pamper," and "Va Va Voom"—and its twenty-four cozy rooms, contact Lisa@skeffington.ie, log on to www.skeffington.ie, or phone +353 (0) 91-563-173. This hotel is known as a man-meeting haunt in itself. It has six bars with live DJs on the weekends.

After Closing. Get some sleep so that you can hit it again the next day. In Galway, the fun never ends!

When Shop Street Turned into Romance Road

The best European man-meeting story I have heard from the pubs on Shop Street came from Miss Masters. Last winter her girlfriend was infatuated with this charming Irish guy that Miss Masters nicknamed "Tempranillo" because he loved drinking that wine with dinner. After meeting him at the University, she tried everything she could think of to get close to him, from planning study sessions to pre-gaming Kings parties. They got to be very good friends, but nothing romantic happened.

Finally, Miss Masters' girlfriend decided to go all out. Since the holiday season is the time for romance and mistletoe was all about, in late December she planned a pub crawl called "The Twelve Pubs of Christmas." She set up the entire event, selected the twelve pubs to party at, got herself ready for romance, and invited Tempranillo and some other friends. Everyone had a wonderful time and Tempranillo was obviously impressed with this girl's creativity. They got much closer during the evening, but still no romance. Well, it turned out that the pub crawl was the pre-game to romance just like having a drink in a bar or playing Kings is the pre-game to clubbing.

After the pub crawl, the group decided to go to their dorms for an intimate get-together instead of going dancing. While they walked back, rain started furiously pouring down. Not having umbrellas, everyone ran for it except Tempranillo, who pulled Miss Masters' friend underneath a balcony and kissed her. About time! She described it as one of those kisses that was really intense. She was soaking wet with her heart pounding as hard as the rain. That was the beginning of the Tempranillo romance. Shop Street should be called Romance Road. Enjoy it!

Italy

In just one trip to this lovely country you can take in twenty-seven centuries of art and architecture, transport yourself to the Renaissance, and find your own Renaissance man. You don't even need to throw your coin in the Trevi Fountain and make a wish to do it. After all, where did Michelangelo get the inspiration for his *David*? So, in addition to feasting on the Pantheon, Sistine Chapel, and Castel Sant'Angelo in Rome, shopping at the storied Mercato Nuovo in Florence, and visiting the Gothic palaces and medieval enclaves of Siena, you can cultivate your taste for Italian men.

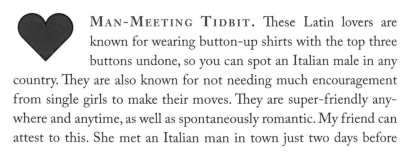 MAN-MEETING TIDBIT. These Latin lovers are known for wearing button-up shirts with the top three buttons undone, so you can spot an Italian male in any country. They are also known for not needing much encouragement from single girls to make their moves. They are super-friendly anywhere and anytime, as well as spontaneously romantic. My friend can attest to this. She met an Italian man in town just two days before

leaving the country. He sent her a text the following night asking her to go out with him. She called him back and explained that she would love to see him again, but unfortunately she couldn't. She was packing and had to be at the airport very early the next morning. Mr. Spontaneous Italian Lover replied, "Meet me in the piazza in ten minutes. Don't think about tomorrow. Once you have met me, it will be too late to say you can't."

When a Broken Heart Mended in Italy

As you can see, in affairs of the heart Italian men are big on acting in the moment. Another friend told a similar story. She met an Italian Artsy in a stunning club. She had just broken up with her boyfriend and temporarily forgot her heartache when mesmerized by this particular stallion. They danced for hours. When he started kissing her, she happily complied. Then she abruptly stopped, explaining, "I'm sorry. I just broke up with my boyfriend. It was a really serious relationship. I shouldn't do this yet." The Italian man replied with a convincing smile, "It's too late to say you shouldn't, because you already have!" During her trip, she was proposed to by three Italian men. So much for her serious relationship . . . that was so last week!

Try out the following locations where single girls have acted in the moment with Italian men and reaped many fun memories.

Florence (Piazza Michelangelo)

Piazza Michelangelo, located on the south bank of the Arno river, is kind of like a park, except no one plays catch or walks dogs. It is exclusively a people-watching outlet, and an amazingly *splendido* one at that. Covered with stones and surrounded by benches and quaint little restaurants, this piazza looks down on the entire city of Florence.

It has an absolutely incredible view. Italians regularly grab coffee or wine and go out to the benches to enjoy the ambiance. Sipping a beverage can become an all-day endeavor once you smell the refreshing European air and meet the men. They fill the piazza from early in the morning until about ten at night.

 MAN-MEETING TIDBIT. The Christmas season is one of the best times to visit Piazza Michelangelo. Then, it is swathed in glowing lights and transformed into an Italian wonderland. Relax and stay awhile. This country is known for having inhabitants who take life at a slow, enjoyable pace. Settle in for the evening and select your favorite Taly. When he heads on over to the nearby gelato store, you do the same. Italians can be quite forward. Your new pursuit is apt to take it from there and go further!

Italy is filled with piazzas. All are enchanting, but Michelangelo is hands down a favorite among single girls.

Florence (Café Rivoire)

Café Rivoire (+39 055 214 412) is an elite café on Piazza della Signoria known for its scrumptious cakes and rich coffee. If you wish to be selected by a high society gent, snack at this scene. Remember, protocol is pertinent. Do not buy your shot of coffee, chug it down at the counter, and charge off. Your Italian lover will not jog after you. Instead, pay the cover charge to have the privilege of sitting at a table. Pay a cover charge just to sit at a table and drink a cup of coffee? You heard me—suck it up and dole out the dollars, or should I say euros? It's not an astronomical amount and you can stay as long as you like without being pressured. After you are invited to the society stud's next big event, you will thank me for this suggestion.

Florence (YAB)

YAB is one of Italy's top clubs. It is equipped with florescent spotlights that make you feel like you are being featured on the catwalk and is found on Via Sassetti, 5/R Firenze (+39 055-215-160). Its name stands for "You Are Beautiful." What girl doesn't want to hear that?!

Ladies are usually let in for free while males have to pay steep fees. You would think that this would scare away the guys, but YAB is actually a rich man's destination. The kind of man who dines at five-star restaurants, houses his yacht in the harbor, and parks his Ferrari in the garage comes to this club. He will use his money to impress you. If you are the sort who succumbs to high-end treatment, step into YAB. You know you are beautiful! If you are not taken by fancy dates, this is not your spot. Leave it to those of us who lack luxury self-control.

When the Girls Were Wined and Dined by Messrs. Lamborghini

To fully understand the type of Italian man who frequents YAB, I want to share a story about my friend's weekend trip to Florence. She and some girlfriends were only in town for a few days. They knew that they didn't have enough time to date the men, they weren't into random play, and they didn't have hookup maps to fill in like the Sexcapader. They just wanted to have fun exploring the town—and fun was definitely what they had! On their first night there, they dined at a nice restaurant next to a table with some eye-catching Italian men. Ten minutes into their meal, the girls received a bottle of fine wine, courtesy of the next table. Ten minutes after that they received flowers from their admirers. And ten minutes after that, the men came over asking for an introduction. They offered to show the girls around town for the rest of the evening. Showing the girls around town would be an understatement. They were escorted to every trendy bar and club in the city, danced in hot spot after hot spot, and sampled the Italian spectrum of exotic drinks.

The next day, the men offered to take the girls in their Lamborghinis to a traditional wine-tasting event before they left town. My friend said that this was one of her most memorable trips. Even though the men knew that the girls' visit was short, they genuinely wanted to show them a good time, and were perfect gentlemen. So whether you are just in town for a weekend or for an extended stay, if you want to up your chances of being entertained by a Mr. Lamborghini in the know, dance on over to YAB. Hopefully you will get to enjoy wine-tasting the next day.

Liguria (Cinque Terre)

The Cinque Terre trail is a hiking pass encompassing five villages: Riomaggiore, Manarola, Corniglia, Vernazza, and Monterosso al Mare. All have little restaurants where you can settle in with the natives for a break while overlooking the stunning sea in a *magnifico* region of Italy called Liguria.

Each of these five villages is accessible by train, so once you have arrived at your starting village go to a **Cinque Terre Trail Pay Station and Information Post**. There you will receive a map on which each village is visibly marked and easy to locate, and you can buy a trail day pass or a card with different options including multi-day deals.

The Scoop on the Five Villages. Hiking from Monterosso to Vernazza usually takes about two hours, from Vernazza to Corniglia is about two more, from Corniglia to Manarola is a one-hour trek, and from Manarola to Riomaggiore is only a twenty-minute walk. But take as much time as you want. Your goal here is to have fun and splurge on European guys, not to get in shape for the Olympics, so there's no need to push yourself.

If you do just want to spend one day blazing the trail, I'd suggest seeing how far you move at a comfortable pace. At dawn, you can always take a train out of wherever you end up. If you want to skip sections of Cinque Terre, you can also take a ferry to another village. This is a wonderful option for having a leisurely break while enjoying your surroundings.

Preplanning your pace is nearly impossible because it depends on which European men you happen upon and their agendas. Monterosso, with its long sandy beach, is the best place to find a native companion. It is fun to have a snuggle buddy under a traditional Italian umbrella while absorbing the sea breeze. By the time you get to Manarola, you can enhance your European liaison with a tête-à-tête at its fabulous swimming spot. The rocks are flat, so now all you have to do is remember to wear your flattering bikini under your cute hiking clothes . . . And getting sidetracked on the trail between Riomaggiore and Manarola is no waste of time. There is an easy route along the coast where the marine aroma and views promote romance. With the name **Via dell'Amore**, I doubt that you will just be hiking with your new Italian man.

Word to the Wise. When planning your trip along the Cinque Terre Trail, feel free to email any questions to info@cinqueterreonline.com.

Rome (Brancaleone and Other Guy-Getting Clubs)

The best clubs in Rome are only frequented by natives and travelers in the know, and you are on the verge of becoming one of them.

 Man-Meeting Tidbit. Before you hear about these clubs, I want to give single girls the inside track on how Roman men check out prospects. This comes straight from my friend, Blondie de Femme, the one who lured in

Constantin Scandiano, the Airbrushed surf instructor with the Dolce & Gabbana underwear. Blondie spent four months in Rome and can assure you that although men from some European regions look first at a girl's butt and others at her boobs, the Romans will judge you by your shoes! These guys are very fashion and quality conscious. Basically, if you want to make a favorable first impression, your shoes had better be appealing times ten—while still being comfortable, that is. Like me, Blondie de Femme wore stylish, comfy Söffts. Her feet were happy and so were the Roman men.

The Storied Brancaleone. Now that you have on your man-attracting shoes, head over to Brancaleone. It is far out from the heart of Rome at Via Levanna 11, 00141 (+39 06-8200-0959), but far out from the city center does not mean far out from the action. This club is the action. Period!

Actually, many clubs that attract Italian men are destinations only for those in the know—either located a ways off from the beaten path or in buildings with no names. In fact, word of mouth is the only way most travelers find out about the hottest of hot spots in Rome. Since most pamphlets clue you in to the exquisite and easy-to-find Roman scenes, like the Colosseum and Pantheon, but leave out the not so easy-to-find clubs filled with Italian men, you could visit this beautiful city and never meet those beautiful Roman males. This is why I'm about to give you the inside track on these hideaways, starting with Brancaleone, a favorite among single girls.

Word to the Wise. But first, since these clubs can be a bit tricky to locate, pick up *Streetwise Rome*. This is a small map the size of a business envelope. It is laminated, foldable, and perfect for letting you know where you are among all the little corners and street-name changes in this city. Of course, *only* use this map if there is not a European male nearby who you would like to meet. In that case, follow Tip #16: Use Getting Lost to Your Advantage, and make it easy for a future prospect to meet you.

Brancaleone is so "in" that you are unlikely to find anyone who is not European inside. This club is known for having a steeper cover charge for those who do not speak Italian well, so this is one time to really brush up on the verbs and let the bouncer know, in Italian, that you will not be pushed into paying extra.

Once inside, file into a room on the left where Italians hang out on couches. This is where everyone mingles in a chill-out environment. Then, all of a sudden, an intense bass will start pounding. It is the cue to hustle with your couch honey to another room, where screens of videos play and everyone dances. The music and rhythms are fabulous and the men really know how to move. Grind is not a step in their dance repertoire. They are more likely to rumba, cha-cha, and tango. But don't think the Italians social dance at a respectable distance. No way! Up close and personal is the Roman persona. So let the bass keep the beat, let your hips move, and let what happens happen.

When Blondie de Femme Taught
Roman Men the Art of the "Shot"

The men at Brancaleone are known for being A-partiers, attractive, and very easygoing. My friends and I found that these "easygoing" characters want to teach you their dance moves and culture as well as experience yours. So be yourself and have fun. If you want to introduce them to something from your country, do it . . . after spending sufficient time appreciating theirs, that is.

Blondie de Femme learned all of the Italian dance moves from the men at Brancaleone and then taught them something from her country. She decided that they were better off not knowing how to grind, but they did need to know how to take shots, which to most

Europeans is a completely foreign concept. So Blondie de Femme hauled her cute little butt from the dance floor to the bar. Of course, the Italian hotties followed her. Once there, she introduced them to the "American shot." It was a hit. Several husky Talies bellied up to the bar to take shots and meet her. After that, she had a shot at every SAM in the club!

Other Guy-Getting Clubs—Supperclub, Coyote, and Gilda. Three other hot Rome dance spots are Supperclub, Coyote, and Gilda.

Supperclub is located on Via dé Nari, 14 00186 (+39 06-6880-7207). It is a "chain" in the sense that there are Supperclubs around Europe and now in America. But don't think this club is filled with Americans or visitors from other regions. It is not even close to a tourist attraction. In fact, there is no sign on the door. The only people who know about this Roman venue are Europeans and a handful of in-the-know travelers from other countries. So now you can be one of them. Don't come to this destination if you are on a budget or in a hurry. There is normally a huge waiting list and it costs a lot to get in. The haunt serves dinner while patrons enjoy performers and dance. This is where you can find the wealthy Italian men who splurge on entertainment.

Coyote is found on Via di Monte Testaccio, 48b, 00153 (+39 340-244-5874). This is where some Slightly Sleazy but ridiculously fun and wacky Italian men hang out. The club has several rooms blasting the very *best* Euro dance music.

Gilda dominates Via Mario de' Fiori, 97, near the Spanish Steps (+39 66-784-8388). It draws in the single business girl's hot ticket—sophisticated young Europeans and Italian politicians—and the single girl's not-so-hot ticket—Italian men with their younger mistresses. Just brush past the latter to get to the wowers. The only annoying aspect of Gilda is the fact that you will have to buy your drink ticket far away from where you actually pick up your drink. But, hey, you might get to add another Italian man to your date card while you make the journey. OK, so I'm exaggerating about the distance, but it is a ways apart.

Word to the Wise/Summer Switch. Many of the clubs in Rome move to Ostia Beach venues during the warm summer. Take the Piramide metro to Termini (main station), then switch to Metro B and stop at Lido Centro to party at Ostia Beach and meet the men while enjoying the sand and surf!

Blonde Girls' Guy-Getting Power. Rome is full of dark-haired, brown-eyed, stunning men. Many are only 5'8" or 5'9", so if you're a petite blonde girl, this is your perfect guy-getting destination. The men here absolutely love blondes—I mean *love*! And the blonder the better (see Tip #8: Opposites Attract). In fact, if you are blonde and on a budget, dine at **Red Rose Café** on Via del Plebiscito. It is known for giving a "Blonde Discount."

Siena (The Tea Room)

The Tea Room (+39 0577-222-753) is a man-meeting haven, especially in winter when the weather is cold. Go to Via di Porta Giustizia 11 to connect with the twenty- to thirty-year-old Siena spectrum. Many of them frequent this haunt as a warm-up to partying the night away. This cozy enclave has low ceilings, brick arches, and what seems like every possible type of tea and cake, plus a huge shelf of board games. The Tea Room is a great place to play games while sipping tea, making new friends, and bonding with old ones. Pick out your board game and players and you are set. But remember, you are always the winner in any game if your enticing opponent becomes more than a friend by the end of the evening!

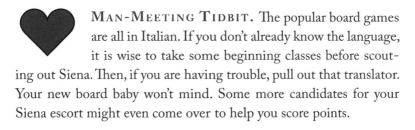

MAN-MEETING TIDBIT. The popular board games are all in Italian. If you don't already know the language, it is wise to take some beginning classes before scouting out Siena. Then, if you are having trouble, pull out that translator. Your new board baby won't mind. Some more candidates for your Siena escort might even come over to help you score points.

When College Girls Were Treated Like Celebrities

Not being proficient in the language won't stop you from meeting men at the Tea Room. In fact, my friend who was a regular there during her Siena stay said that having a non-Italian accent draws in the men. She and her friends were from the States and still learning the language. The natives thought their accents were so charming that every time the girls visited this hub, they gathered around their table wanting to meet them. My friend said she felt like a movie star at an autograph signing, minus the fact that she didn't have to sign her name . . . she just had to keep telling it to her admiring European prospects. The owner of the Tea Room was also smitten with the girls, their broken Italian, and their American accents. He frequently brought them complimentary desserts that were set on fire, making cool designs. So just learn the language to the best of your ability and let your lack of pronunciation lure in the men.

Word to the Wise. The Tea Room is known for filling up fast. It is wise to make reservations the day before.

Multiple Towns (Granfondo Pinarello)

Want to compete beside the legendary European cyclists? If you think you can keep up, then go to www.granfondopinarello.com/eng/index .php to find out about registering for the Granfondo (+39 0422-420-877). It features multiple events in multiple cities throughout Italy.

Granfondo races are typically about 160–225 kilometers long and sometimes offer a *medio fondo*, which is normally under 120 kilometers, for those who aren't as physically fit. When it comes to cycling, I'm totally all about the medio fondo. Actually, I probably wouldn't even last that long there. Joining the vivacious spectators on the sidelines is within my comfort zone, but being a buff biking babe is clearly the best approach, because you might get to ride beside the pros. These races are covered by major cycling magazines and spotlight the sponsored riders. You know . . . the kind of European guys who spend all day on their bikes and have amazing muscles to prove it.

For major Granfondo races, entry fees typically range between twenty and forty euros and cover the cost of mechanical and medical support and food along the way. Many events also provide coupons for the post-competition pasta party—the ideal time to become intimate with those prime racers and their well-toned bods. Some of the smaller events only cost a few euros, but obviously come with less perks.

Word to the Wise. Dates and locations of the Grandfondo vary and you must sign up for some options months in advance, so keep checking the website and get yourself in spandex-wearing shape.

Portugal

Portugal is one of the smallest European countries with one of the fastest-growing economics. Lisbon, the capital, is quickly becoming cosmopolitan while at the same time holding on to its ancient past. In the Baixa district some of the downtown streets have been closed to motor vehicles and lined with cobblestones. Artisans have moved in and pedestrian malls have been created, so this is the perfect place to go shopping and get your local flair. If a Portugese man is on your shopping list, after you have done in Baixa head on over to Barrio Alto.

MAN-MEETING TIDBIT. But before you do, you will be happy to hear that these men are known for being very polite and all about wine and fish. So eat it up! I have never been to Lisbon, but my girlfriend wanted me to give the single gals the details on the guys' looks. They are tan, dark-eyed, and very attractive, but pretty hairy . . . everywhere. Some girls love that amount of testosterone, so if you do, then Lisbon is where it's at.

Lisbon (Barrio Alto)

Barrio Alto is perched atop a hilly peak and is one of the few areas untouched by the devastating 1755 earthquake. Previously home to a noble neighborhood, some of the original houses, including estates with adjoining chapels, are still in use. The district has a distinctively dual personality. During the day, it is flooded with families. Then, at night, the Portuguese social potion sets in and the bars and restaurants that are invisible in the sunlight become lively landmarks.

Toss your plans overboard when you enter Barrio Alto. Let the wind take you to any or all of the tiny bars. Many are only the size of college dorm rooms. Crazy partiers grab drinks and greet each other on the street outside. You know that grabbing drinks means you can take advantage of Tips #27 and #28: Pause When Ordering a Drink and The Last Sips of Your Drink Are Pivotal. Everyone is in a mingling mood, so your results should be mantastic.

All types of men from Lisbon come to this hot spot exclusively to meet girls. They say that it is the most awesome European pick-up point. If the male species thinks it's awesome so will you, because that means there will be guys galore!

Word to the Wise. Anywhere you go in Portugal, if you see a bar that says "Bar" on the entrance, it means that the establishment is sketchy. There are quite a few "Bars" dotting this country and they attract men who are more than Slightly Sleazy.

When Betsey Got Down in a "Bar"

My friend Betsey, the professional burlesque dancer who fell in love with the Italian romantic, discovered this and had quite the "Bar" experience on her first trip to Portugal. She was there performing at a 1920s-feeling club. One night after their performance, the troupe was very thirsty and wanted to stop for a drink. Naturally, when they saw the word "Bar" they entered. What happened after that was an evening never to be forgotten.

To appropriately paint the picture, this "Bar" didn't really have a door . . . just a piece of carpet. But being parched, my friend and her performance troupe didn't think much about it. They proceeded inside to find that all of the walls were also carpeted. The bartenders didn't speak English. Betsey asked for a screwdriver. Instead of getting vodka and orange juice, she got straight vodka with a little orange juice on the side. Who knew straight vodka quenched a thirst? Someone's thirst at a "Bar," perhaps. So Betsey and her friends were chilling, minding their own business, when an English-speaking man approached and asked, "Do you know where you are?" Being astute, Betsey replied, "In a bar." Not so much. The man explained, "You are in a brothel." Betsey, a girl who makes fun everywhere, said, "I know how to get down." She figured, "Hey, so I'm in a brothel. I'm going to have a great time." She showed everyone that the ladies of the night had nothing on her sexy dance moves.

Lisbon (Chapitô)

If you want to dine and be richly entertained while meeting enthralling Portuguese men, Betsey highly recommends Chapitô, located at Rua Costa do Castelo 7 in the historical part of Lisbon (+351 21 885-5550). This jewel is hidden in an out-of-the-way spot some distance from the heart of the city, but it is definitely worth the trek . . . and it is not hidden from the European men. Once you wind up the hill with its beautiful castle you will be ready for Chapitô's enchantments. You can come here day or night and order just a beverage or get a full meal. I hear that sunset is the prime time. The restaurant has an outdoor terrace where you can gaze at the gorgeous gardens and river as the sun melts into the horizon.

♥ MAN-MEETING TIDBIT. Indoors, the feel of Chapitô is bohemian. It attracts men of a variety of age ranges, but especially those in their twenties. This haunt is buzzing with friendly, merry Europeans, but Artsy gents seem to especially love the live music and performances that this venue is known for.

Betsey said the voices of many Portuguese singers there are so amazing that they "make you want to cry." That would make sense since Chapitô also houses the Professional School of Arts and Crafts. Because the restaurant is so isolated, the performers began teaching each other between shows. Now they have a complete school. Not only do they teach singing and acting, but circus acrobatics as well. You can enjoy their acumen on the high wire while savoring your meal and the men.

Word to the Wise. For further information on this destination, go to www.chapito.org. If you don't speak the language, use Google's translator. Then click on "House Chapitô" followed by "Barty" for the details on this haunt's bar and "Restô" if you want a meal. The website also gives the dates and times that the hot spot is open.

Scotland

Scotland, where the royal family famously summers, is a country steeped in stories of heroes and romance. Robert Louis Stevenson and Mary, Queen of Scots, in different eras, walked the same city streets and shared the same heather-cloaked highland hills. *Britannia*, the famous royal yacht, sailed into the harbor and stayed. If you want to sail off with an appealing Scot, you should find success at the Edinburgh Festival and Hogmanay.

MAN-MEETING TIDBIT. Before you set sail, my girlfriends who have visited this country want to let you know that the Scot's accents can be very difficult to understand at first, but it's worth making the effort to get over this hurdle.

When Miss Athletic Traveler Met Mr. Intriguing Scot

One of my athletic American girlfriends who went on a weekend hike in Scotland can attest to the language barrier. When she arrived at her lodge, she learned that her reservation had been mixed up. Instead of staying with other female hikers, she was put in a room with five Scottish men. Miss Athletic Traveler was especially intrigued by one of them, but she could not understand a word any of them said. Their accents were so thick that she thought they were speaking a foreign language. She asked them what language they spoke and was stunned when they replied, "English." That was English? Well, it was news to her. As the weekend went on, she started to understand them more and more until finally communication was no longer an issue.

Miss Athletic Traveler learned that Mr. Intriguing Scot was even more intriguing when she could experience his entertaining wit. They started dating. He visited her at other European locations. When she returned to the US, he refused to break off the relationship. She got a work visa to join him in Scotland for eight months. When that expired, he got a work visa to join her in the States. They have continued seeing each other for four years, taking turns visiting the other's homeland.

One of Miss Athletic Traveler's treasured memories is when they went to Hawaii. Her Scot had never seen palm trees before. He was so enthralled with them that he started taking pictures in the airport. She says if you speak English and are having a hard time understanding a Scot, just show him a picture of a palm tree and he will love you. Then relax and realize that conversation will come as you learn to decipher the words cloaked in his thick Scottish brogue.

Edinburgh (Edinburgh Festival)

The Edinburgh Festival (+44 (0) 131-473-2000 for reservations; +44 (0) 131-473-2099 for information) is held every year for three weeks at the end of summer. Scotland's brightest weather is during this time of year. It enhances the fresh greenery of this emerald city, and sets off the castle-style buildings and Edinburgh's famous historic palace that hosts visitors like you. This festival is actually a collection of several simultaneous festivals, which provides a vast selection of entertainment, including classical music, theater, opera, dance, and art. The best cutting-edge trends, the most popular choreography, and the latest crafty creations are all showcased at the Edinburgh Festival. And it doesn't just feature Scottish talent. Exhibitors come from around the world. Naturally, Edinburgh holds the world's record for staging the largest art showing. This means that it also holds the world's record for attracting the largest number of sage Scots, not to mention hosts of other eligible men from other countries . . . with an abundance of Artsy gents.

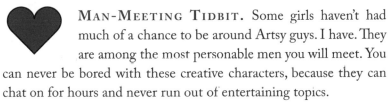

MAN-MEETING TIDBIT. Some girls haven't had much of a chance to be around Artsy guys. I have. They are among the most personable men you will meet. You can never be bored with these creative characters, because they can chat on for hours and never run out of entertaining topics.

One of my girlfriends from the States who is a dancer performed at the Edinburgh Festival. She described it as a "man-meeting extravaganza!" She was there for all three weeks. Every day, people were in a party mood and into making new friends.

Word to the Wise. For the festival calendar, ticket prices, and booking arrangements log on to www.eif.co.uk and plan ahead.

Edinburgh (Hogmanay)

Hogmanay (+44 (0) 844-894-2010), which means "great love day" in old Scandinavian, celebrates Scotland's Viking era along with the end of each year and the beginning of the next. This is not just one day of Scottish lovin', but four days of fantastic Edinburgh events. I would gamble that this happening is hands down one of the most exciting ways to ring out the old year and bring in the new.

The festivities run from December 29 through January 1. That gives you two whole days to decide which lucky Scot you will let have the privilege of sharing a midnight New Year's kiss. Don't sell yourself short. Go for the man who treats you the best. It is said that your love life for the following year will mimic that midnight moment. He had better act like a prince, because you deserve to be treated like a princess for the next 365 days. Here are the typical activities leading up to that pivotal point.

December 29 is the day to scout out your surroundings. Attend the torchlight procession, which is led by the Vikings and dramatically ends at Calton Hill. There, an authentic replica of a longship receives a symbolic burial in a splendor of fire.

December 30 is the time to hook your hottie. And what better place is there than a traditional Celtic party accompanied by music, storytelling, and comedic acts?

December 31 is the date to reel him in. This is when Edinburgh's Hogmanay Street Party kicks off. Onstage entertainment, fireworks, and hundreds of thousands of partygoers are just a few of the selling features. There are several other ticketed events to choose from, including extravaganzas involving Celtic bands and pipers, and various dance gatherings. It's just too much fun for one night!

January 1 is the Edinburgh Triathlon. If you have the stamina to roll out of bed, you can work off the weight you gained during the last three days of indulgence and meet more European men. After swimming, cycling, and running, your body will be back in its man-alluring state.

Word to the Wise. Getting last minute passes to the New Year's Eve Street Party and other festival events can be quite tricky, if not impossible. Plan early. Go to www.edinburghshogmanay.com and purchase your tickets way before the celebration. Then put on that party pizzazz—you're being hosted by Hogmanay!

Slovenia

A little knowledge of the history of Slovenia will go a long way in helping you understand why Metelkova is *the* man-meeting hub in this country, how this improbable hot spot came to be, and the mentality of the Slovene male.

Slovenians are resourceful, resilient, and determined. In the 1500s, this small country became part of a kingdom that included Austria and Hungary. Following the collapse of this empire in World War I, Slovenia declared its independence and joined other nations to form Yugoslavia. During World War II, the Nazis invaded this new nation and divided Slovenia among Germany, Italy, and Hungary, but the Slovenes cleverly chose to ignore this. They even fought their own guerilla war against the Nazis with much success. When World War II ended, Slovenia was strong-armed into the new Communist nation of Yugoslavia, but those resourceful Slovenes did not accept that either and managed to gain their independence with relatively little violence. In one of the most remarkable success stories in Europe, they joined the European Union and NATO, prospered, and even became the first former Communist nation to preside over the EU. So, based upon five hundred years of history, Slovenians could be called "slick rebels."

This country is built on top of thousands of incredible caves. The city to visit is Ljubljana, the capital. The nightlife there is fantastic, and one in ten inhabitants is a student, so there are an abundance of artsy enclaves and trendy cafés—but the no-miss Slovenian stop for every single girl is Metelkova.

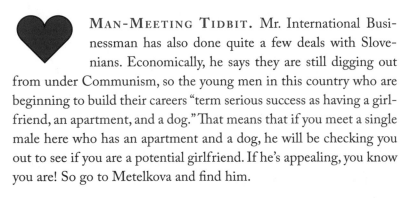 MAN-MEETING TIDBIT. Mr. International Businessman has also done quite a few deals with Slovenians. Economically, he says they are still digging out from under Communism, so the young men in this country who are beginning to build their careers "term serious success as having a girlfriend, an apartment, and a dog." That means that if you meet a single male here who has an apartment and a dog, he will be checking you out to see if you are a potential girlfriend. If he's appealing, you know you are! So go to Metelkova and find him.

Ljubljana (Metelkova)

Metelkova is a bohemian blessing. This area was once a military barracks for the Yugoslav army. They moved out in 1991. Then the neighborhood was taken over by squatters who paid no mind to the fact that they didn't have the rights to the land. They went forward opening stores, restaurants, bars, and hostels, and creating their own unique culture.

Every year, the Slovenian government threatens to kick them out. Wrecking balls and tractors have even been brought in to destroy the settlement, but the government has yet to act. You may be thinking that this is a really cool story, but what does it have to do with meeting European men? Today, Metelkova is a hopping, alternative, avant-garde hub where tons of sixteen- to thirty-year-old guys crowd in to party.

One of the most popular places in town is **Hostel Celica**, which is found on Metelkova 8, 1000 Ljubljana (+386 (0) 1-230-9700). This is a hot spot in and of itself, acclaimed as one of the hippest haunts in Europe. It was once a military jail. Today most of the cells have been converted into rooms. There are also a few bars, which are crawling with native men and adventurous European travelers. Once you have seen the bright exterior shouting in pink, purple, yellow, orange, and red, you will understand why it is the mainstay of the Metelkova neighborhood and such a draw. Log on to www.hostelcelica.com to book your stay.

Word to the Wise. Moving in on this opportunity as quickly as possible is a good idea. Although I really hope the Slovenian government never comes through with their threat to destroy this impromptu hot spot, it's impossible to know what will happen.

Spain

When Franco died and Spain was freed from his grasp, this country was emancipated and for most the celebration has never stopped. With its strategic position abutting the Atlantic Ocean, Mediterranean Sea, and Strait of Gibraltar, Spain has a long, rich history as a welcome crossroads among nations and as a leader in art, architecture, cuisine, and culture. This tradition, which was put on hold during Franco's reign, has been in full swing ever since. Today, Spain is simply a great place to meet European men from a variety of countries. Whether you love sports, bars and clubs, or festivals, I have found places where you will definitely find them.

I have spent about four months in Spain and traveled throughout the country. It is amazing! Parties, festivals, and clubs normally don't get going until about 1:30 AM and continue all night. In the cities, long weekend afternoon siestas are the key to enjoying Spanish nights and Spanish men.

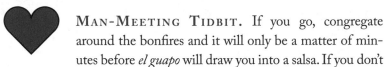 **MAN-MEETING TIDBIT.** I have found Spaniards among the friendliest of European males. They go out of their way to help everyone—but especially single girls. A typical example occurred when I studied at the Complutense University of Madrid. I was trying to get something out of a vending machine that only took exact change. The machine didn't actually say this, so I didn't understand why it wasn't working. A Spaniard noticed, came over, and showed me how to use it. When he realized that I didn't have exact change, he said, "Don't worry, I've got it covered." When I told him it was really nice of him to come over and help me, he said, "That's just how we are here." All of my friends were helped by Spaniards when they found themselves in predicaments that ranged from trying to find a lost passport to getting lost themselves to being unable to operate a copy machine. Each time the men graciously volunteered their assistance.

Barcelona (The Festival of San Juan)

Barcelona's Festival of San Juan is a *noche* to remember for a lifetime. On Summer Solstice, the entire town piles onto the beach for fireworks, enormous bonfires, bands, and dancing. When we went, it was so crowded that we often couldn't see the sand.

MAN-MEETING TIDBIT. If you go, congregate around the bonfires and it will only be a matter of minutes before *el guapo* will draw you into a salsa. If you don't know the steps, he will gladly teach you. But be forewarned, the single Spaniards have a way of turning an innocent salsa into a steamy seduction! Around 4 AM, when the festival starts to die down, all of the beach clubs will be in full swing. If you want to keep celebrating, fiesta until about 8 AM. Then you can grab some breakfast and rest the day away. Good thing you are already at the beach. Have your bikini packed in your purse or wear it underneath your clothes and you won't have to leave. Just get some rays, relax those dancing feet, and soak in the sea.

The Feel of the Festival. The Barcelona festival has an extremely inviting feel. It not only attracts singles, but also families, grandparents, and great grandparents. The older generations stay out partying until about 3 AM! This is their version of turning in early, since the festivities last all night long.

Native festival attendees really want to make sure that everyone has a bang-up time. They never like to see any girl not dancing around the campfire, so if a wife notices that you are standing all alone it is not uncommon for her to ask her husband to dance with you for one song. Don't turn him down because he is married. You would come off as ungrateful. Such a couple is only being hospitable. When the husband dances with you, there will be lots of twirling. You won't be standing close in the least. Think about the way you would dance with your dad and you get the perfect visual. My friends and I danced with everyone—stunning single men, little kids, sweet husbands, grandfathers, and great grandfathers.

Caveat. While you are enjoying the dancing and camaraderie, know that children—and older single guys who can act like children on this night of the year—love firecrackers. On Summer Solstice they will set them off everywhere around the town and at the festival, so just be on the lookout. You could be walking and see several firecrackers literally explode just inches from you.

When Wearing Sunglasses at Night Was a Man Magnet

I didn't want to get sparks in my face or smoke from the huge bonfires in my eyes, so I wore a pair of those trendy oversized sunglasses. They may have been trendy during the day when the sun was out, but at night, obviously no one else was wearing them. My friend said that everyone would think I looked ridiculous if I wore them. I told her that she could walk in front of me and pretend she didn't know me.

Well, the sunglasses oddly turned into a way of meeting men. I heard so many friendly voices shouting out in Spanish, "Blondie, watch out for the sun!" Remember, in Spain I'm considered a blonde. When the guys found out that the firecrackers scared me, they were extremely comforting, offering to protect me the entire night. My friend grabbed my sunglasses and said, "I want to meet the men. Give me those." Do you think maybe she had a little change of heart?

So if you scare easy like me and want to protect your face from sparks and smoke, don't worry about what your friends say and wear sunglasses. What I especially love about these Spaniards is that they are the opposite of judgmental. So be yourself and do what makes you feel happy. The Spaniards will appreciate you for this and want to meet you.

The Meaning of the Festival. There are two meanings for this festival—the traditional one and the one ascribed to it by the locals. The traditional meaning is one of renewal. In keeping with this, Spaniards jump over fires. This symbolizes the renewal of their bodies and souls. Then they dip in the sea to wash away any evil spirits. I saw people dipping in the sea, but I only saw a few jumping over fires. The word around town was that if you wrote three wishes, each one on a separate piece of paper, and burned them in a bonfire at the festival, they would come true before the next Summer Solstice. Many festival-goers did this but I have never read about it anywhere—I want to let you in on what really happens. Go to the Festival of San Juan and see if you can make your man-meeting wishes come true!

Fashion Flash. This is one place where you should not wear your fancy clothes. Festivals have a funky, casual feel. When I attended, I was on a weekend trip to Barcelona. I didn't even know about the festival until I arrived, and the only casual clothes I brought were jeans and pajamas. My PJ top was from the Pink Collection at Victoria's Secret. It had polka dots and read, "My Dog is the Cutest." I went ahead and wore it, and found that it was actually quite a conversation-opener. A lot of men asked me to translate it for them. I know I said that wearing the foreign fashion is normally the way to go, but this festival is a rare instance where wearing something unique pays off. The goal here is to stand out among the throngs of people.

When Subway Crowd-surfing Kept Me Safe

Subway cars headed to the festival are often so crowded that you can get smushed. There is a lot of pushing and shoving on board to try and fit everyone in. No harm whatsoever is meant, but the experience can be kind of scary. As I've confessed, I'm a scaredy-cat to the core, so while I am getting concerned others might just be thinking, "It's party time!" My girlfriend and I didn't get on the subway until about 1:30 AM, when the festival was cranked up and so were the subways. So many people were jammed into them that some were literally on top of each other. The only riders with breathing room were the ones in the seats, which were completely full. In fact, most of them had two occupants with girls sitting on guys' laps . . . whether they knew the guys or not. Well, they got to know them pretty quickly that way.

What really impressed me about Barcelona was how nice the men were when they sensed that someone needed help. I guess I was looking kind of afraid as I was being pushed here and there on the subway. My very athletic girlfriend told me, "You just have to flex your muscles so that you don't get pushed easily." No amount of flexing was going to stop me from feeling like a boat tossed at sea in a big storm. Noticing this, a Spaniard gave up his seat for me. Talk about a gentleman!

When the subway arrived at the festival, everyone exited like a herd of stampeding buffalo. They were all hoping to get out before the doors closed. The Spaniard who gave up his seat for me came to my rescue once again. He was a tall man so he effortlessly picked me up and passed me over the crowd to a friend. That was my crowd-surfing subway experience. I was so glad that I bypassed, or should I say, passed over, the entire stampede. Meanwhile, my muscular girl-friend's flexing theory failed her. Someone accidentally stepped on her foot and sent her sprawling on the ground under other people's feet. She was OK, minus a swollen ankle.

Word to the Wise. Do not let concern over getting trampled cause you to miss the festival. Instead, take the subway to the beach earlier in the evening before the throngs converge. Then enjoy a relaxing din-ner at a waterfront restaurant before the crazy festivities set in. The beach eateries are charming. My girlfriend and I blazed the Summer Solstice trail so you don't have to learn the no-trample tip the hard way like we did.

Madrid (Kapital)

If you are into clubbing, Kapital is total *paraíso*. It has taken up resi-dence in an old theater on Calle de Atocha 125 (+34 914-202-906). This was where I had my Scarlett O'Hara experience with all of the men lining up to dance with me and where girls with light features score the most Spanish men. Even though much of Spain brings in many travelers from a variety of European countries, I noticed that Kapital had an especially high concentration of Spaniards.

Each of the seven floors in this club features a different type of music and its own distinct extravagant interior. I could seriously stare at the chandeliers for hours. Everything except the plain exterior is absolutely gorgeous, including the men. So don't be deterred by the outside of this club; step inside and you won't regret it.

If you want to take a break from dancing, Kapital has an incredible lounge with a waterfall and exotic drinks, as well as a stage that showcases performers as the audience watches surrounded by gigantic bubbles and fog. There is also a theater where you can "watch" movies. Nobody in there is ever watching . . . if you know what I mean.

Fashion Flash. Be sure to dress up for your Kapital adventure. The bouncer has been known to reject individuals in jeans and flip flops.

Madrid (Palacio Gaviria)

Wouldn't you love to have a *gran fiesta* in Palacio Real, Madrid's magnificent palace where monarchs have held court? This royal domain is appointed with carved mirrors, elegant staircases, and gold trim. There is a club in this city that is a miniature version of Palacio Real complete with ornate regalia fit for coronations. It is called Palacio Gaviria and can be found on Calle de Arenal 9, 28013 (+34 915-266-069). Although the interior architecture looks straight out of the Renaissance, the acoustics and musical selection fit our modern era, and each room is decorated to suit a different dance style.

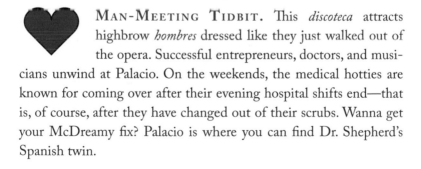 MAN-MEETING TIDBIT. This *discoteca* attracts highbrow *hombres* dressed like they just walked out of the opera. Successful entrepreneurs, doctors, and musicians unwind at Palacio. On the weekends, the medical hotties are known for coming over after their evening hospital shifts end—that is, of course, after they have changed out of their scrubs. Wanna get your McDreamy fix? Palacio is where you can find Dr. Shepherd's Spanish twin.

Fashion Flash. If your desire is to be asked out by these hunks, drape yourself in a dress. Anything colorful or gold-based to match the palace décor is ideal. Like Kapital, you will not be allowed inside if you aren't clothed in nice attire. Also like Kapital, the exterior of Palacio is nothing compared to the interior.

When I Tripped Over Enrique the Rock Star

I met Enrique here. He was the one from Tip #18 (Be Upbeat) who came to my rescue after we left the club to hail a cab. Once we stepped onto the street, we were caught up in a rambunctious festival in full swing with no cabs in sight.

Enrique was my favorite Collegiate Rock Star. He attended Italy's best music conservatory, but was interning in Madrid for the summer. He had this curly dark hair, chocolate brown eyes, a thick accent, and a gentleman's charm. His face looked like he could fit in at the royal palace among the princes, while his choice of dress was ultra-trendy with a funky flare . . . think male Guess model.

When I pseudo-met Enrique, I was busy chatting with my fun but feisty girlfriend while walking down the hall from one exquisitely decorated room to another. I didn't see Enrique sitting on a chair as I tripped over his feet, heading down headfirst. Well, I got a chance to gaze at this gorgeous guy as he caught me. Pretty embarrassed, I hustled my friend into the next room, but Enrique followed us. I really did want to meet him, but I was still humiliated so I sought out a third location. After a couple of minutes, lo and behold, there was Enrique. My girlfriend whispered, "I think he is sending you the message that he wants to meet you." I figured if he wanted to meet me he could introduce himself, but my girlfriend said he needed a little encouragement. Unlike most Italians, he was a little shy.

Following the advice of Tip #31, Miss Initiator started dancing with me to attract Enrique's attention while slowly moving toward him. After a couple of minutes, the Rock Star moved closer until we were only a couple of feet apart. My friend again whispered to me, "This is ridiculous" and gave me a huge shove in her lovable, spirited manner, which sent me smacking into Enrique's chest. My first thought was, "Wow! This guy is even more gorgeous up close." My second thought was, "Now I have more of a reason to be embarrassed." There was no escape. He asked me to dance and we didn't change partners all night.

Good Luck Secret. For single girls, it is good luck to kiss a European man in front of Palacio's velvet chair, which looks fit for a queen. You can find it placed at an angle to the stage and through the door from the largest gold-trimmed mirror. While you kiss your European sweetheart, make a wish befitting a queen. My friend apparently wanted to make a lot of wishes the night that I met Enrique there. She kissed three different European men in this good luck spot!

Morning Ritual. Like all clubs in this country, Palacio stays open and lively until morning. Don't be a deadhead. Dance the night away—that is, unless you have to get up early for something important. About 6 AM is when the Spaniards move the party from Palacio to **San Ginés,** a *chocolatería* serving *churros con chocolate* for breakfast. It is located at No 5, Pasadizo San Ginés (+34 913-656-546). Follow the pack. The chocolatería workers are known for being out-of-this-universe attractive. Well, at that hour everything looks so *bonito,* especially after drinking the very strong Spanish hot chocolate. But honestly, the servers are sizzling. When in Madrid, do as the Madrilaños do. After tripping the light fandango Friday night, most don't return home until at least nine the next morning—an excellent time for an extra-long weekend siesta!

Mallorca (Biking Routes)

Mallorca is like Hollywood for bikers . . . and there you can actually mingle with the celebrities of the European biking world. Say you want to get to know the celluloid stars. Traveling to Hollywood is probably not going to get you any closer to them than you would be when you see them on the big screen. Seriously, I have two friends who spent a Kiefer Sutherland Week in California. They visited all his favorite haunts. They even bought a map to the stars' homes and drove by his house, but they never saw Kiefer.

On the other hand, if you are a biking aficionado, by traveling to Mallorca you can almost lock handlebars with your favorite superstars of the European cycling world and see what goes on behind the scenes in those televised races. Three favorite formulas for two-wheeled guy-getting involve the following terrains: Palmanova-Santa Ponsa, Parque de S' Albura, and Bahia de Pollensa.

Palmanova-Santa Ponsa is a great route for R&R. The paths are very strenuous but they weave through rich beaches where a girl can rejuvenate.

Parque de S'Albura is romance road with an abundance of chirping melodies. There are even hideaway haunts where you can admire the birds on your lovers' escape.

Bahia de Pollensa is a very rigorous route. It is important to bear in mind that the more difficult the trail, the higher the possibility you will run—or should I say wheel—into your favorite biking star.

Pamplona (The Festival of San Fermín)

Starting on July 6 at noon and ending July 14 at midnight, men from all over Europe flock to Pamplona to run with the bulls at the Festival of San Fermín. You may be tempted to jump in and join them—after all, where else will you find so much testosterone in such a confined area? Please refrain! Dodging six bulls that are bearing down on you is not the opportune moment to flirt with your future European *amante*. Watch the race from afar and wait to draw in the men until you are enjoying a drink in the courtyard with the string quartettes.

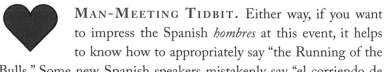 **MAN-MEETING TIDBIT.** Either way, if you want to impress the Spanish *hombres* at this event, it helps to know how to appropriately say "the Running of the Bulls." Some new Spanish speakers mistakenly say "el corriendo de los toros." Even though *corriendo* does mean "running," this is not the correct word to use here. Instead say "el encierro de los toros." *Encierro* literally means "shutting in." In this event, Spaniards focus on the shutting in of the bulls, whereas travelers often focus on when the bulls are let loose and run. A fluent Spanish speaker taught me this phrase and I have used it ever since. When I do, the Spanish men are always appreciative that I cared enough to learn their lingo. Even if you can't speak Spanish, by saying these words, you can win over a Spanish man!

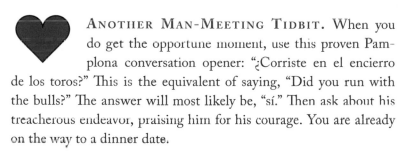 **ANOTHER MAN-MEETING TIDBIT.** When you do get the opportune moment, use this proven Pamplona conversation opener: "¿Corriste en el encierro de los toros?" This is the equivalent of saying, "Did you run with the bulls?" The answer will most likely be, "sí." Then ask about his treacherous endeavor, praising him for his courage. You are already on the way to a dinner date.

Word to the Wise. If you plan to experience the entire festival, book a room way in advance. Log on to http://en.venere.com/hotels_pamplona/?ref=4488 to view your hotel options. If you just want a festive day excursion, you can take a train to town.

Valencia (Las Fallas)

OK, so there are officially a million festivals in this country. If anyone knows how to party, it's the Spaniards. They pride themselves on their crazy fiestas and strive to make each one even more insanely fun than the last.

Las Fallas is the rowdiest festival of them all. This is kind of ironic seeing that it is staged in the normally quiet town of Valencia. If you're into hard partiers and spectacular pyrotechnics, make it a priority to plan your trip there for March 19, when the town swells to three times its usual size. During the day there are lots of activities like parades, bullfights, and pageants. In the evening, fit men stuff fireworks into more than three hundred gigantic statues built specifically for the festival and strategically placed about the city. Just watching those guys labor is a show in and of itself. *¡Ay caramba!* But this is only the warm-up act.

The statues, known as *ninots*, are so large that they must be transported with cranes. At precisely midnight, the street lights are shut off, the crowd chants at the top of its lungs, and all of the ninots are set off in a blaze of fire and smoke. "Extremamente ridículo" is all I have to say! What a way to celebrate the coming of spring.

Sweden

Sweden is famous for being neutral and laid-back. Because it did not take sides in world wars, it was not ravaged like other European nations. As a result, this beautiful Scandinavian country has preserved seven centuries of art and architecture. Today it is mixed with some of the most acclaimed modern steel-and-glass structures. The Swedish city to visit is Stockholm, which is built on fourteen islands linked by bridges, anchored with cobblestone squares, and topped with towers and steeples.

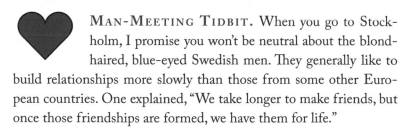 MAN-MEETING TIDBIT. When you go to Stockholm, I promise you won't be neutral about the blond-haired, blue-eyed Swedish men. They generally like to build relationships more slowly than those from some other European countries. One explained, "We take longer to make friends, but once those friendships are formed, we have them for life."

When Londrea Made a Swiss Friend for Life

Swiss men, especially, want to make sure their friends have top-rung Swedish experiences. One of my girlfriends told me a story that perfectly illustrates this point. It's Londrea, the cute climber from Tip #39: Serious Dating, who now lives in London and has the Brit boyfriend. Before she moved to Europe, her boss gave her a spontaneous break after she completed an extremely difficult project. She loved skiing and had a guy friend who lived in Sweden. This was strictly a platonic relationship. The airfare and lift tickets were super low so she decided to visit him. Londrea's Swedish friend was happy to have her come and so was his wife, even though she was gigantically pregnant and looked as if she was about to give birth any minute.

When Londrea arrived, the lady went into labor . . . bad timing! Londrea told them both not to worry about her because she could go skiing while her friend took care of his sweetheart and new baby. Since Londrea made this trip on the spur of the moment, she didn't take the time to check the weather forecast. It was miserable. The snow was slushy and no one was on the slopes except her. Unfortunately, when there are no men, there is no way you can use the chairlift to your man-meeting advantage. Later, Londrea found out that the ticket prices were so low due to the bad weather.

Her male Swedish friend didn't realize her predicament, being preoccupied juggling the needs of his pregnant honey and his responsibilities at work. I can visualize this one. My cousin's wife just gave birth. My family sent them a box of chocolates a few weeks before she went into labor. When he thanked us for it, he added that his appreciation was mostly secondhand, explaining, "It's easier to fight off a grizzly bear than get between a pregnant woman and a box of chocolates!" He would know. He's an avid outdoorsman.

Well, after a few hours on the slopes Londrea was thoroughly wet, cold, and suffering from travel doldrums. She told her Swedish friend that this was the worst trip of her life. She wasn't meaning to be rude. She just felt so nasty that tact flew out the window. This male Swedish sweetie felt so bad that he got together a group of friends and planned a party for Londrea. Then he ran between the hospital and the party, alternately checking on his wife and new baby and Londrea. She had a fabulous time, the wife felt well taken care of, the baby was healthy and happy, and Londrea learned that Swedish men really do care about the friendships they have worked hard to slowly build. She also learned that it is important to check the weather before planning a skiing trip, and that visiting a pregnant lady close to her labor day is a no-go no matter how accommodating she wants to be.

During good weather, I have heard that the skiing in Sweden is mantastic, but I want to focus on a particular non-sports hot spot. This is a place where single girls have told me they not only formed relationships with Swedish men, but with other males. It is an area around the Stockholm Royal Palace where you can be treated royally.

Stockholm
(The Royal Palace Grounds)

The Stockholm Royal Palace is located in the center of the city at Skeppsbron 11130. It is not like many palaces in other countries that are exclusively tourist attractions, or occasionally partially inhabited by some members of the royal family. The exquisitely ornate Stockholm Royal Palace is the residence of a real king, Carl XVI Gustaf, who rules from the largest palace in the world.

The area surrounding the palace is a favorite place for people to mingle, especially during the Changing of the Guard. Many of them are European travelers from other countries. So while you are trying to catch a glimpse of Gustaf, you can do more than just catch glimpses of enticing European men. Here is where you can start building your firm foundation for a relationship. And if it is with a Swede, you know the foundation will be as strong as the Stockholm Royal Palace walls.

When Princess Bride Ran into the One

The Changing of the Guard is where my girlfriend who wanted to fall in love with a European man lured in "the one." On the first night of her weekend visit to Sweden, she and a friend checked into a hostel. She decided to take a shower to wash off her travel grime. The bathroom was coed, but what she didn't realize was that the panels dividing the showers were made of completely see-through glass. She walked into her stall, grabbed her shampoo, started sudsing her hair, and was shocked to see everyone else doing the same. She definitely was not a prude, but who wouldn't be surprised at being able to wave at your shower buddies?

My friend grabbed her towel, ran out of the shower, and crashed into a German male traveler who was on his way into the bathroom. It was like love at first sight. They stared into each other's eyes until my friend realized that she was dripping wet, still had suds in her hair, and hadn't gotten rid of her travel grime . . . but love doesn't care about such little details. Embarrassed, my friend scurried off. She came back and tried the shower experience again later when there weren't any bathroom buddies.

The next day, the Princess Bride went to the Changing of the Guard at the Stockholm Royal Palace. Surprise! Suddenly Mr. Shower Man was standing next to her. He was even more infatuated when he saw my friend post-shower and sudsless. She was still embarrassed, but he refused to let her escape again. A benefit of the forthright nature of Germans is that if they like you, they won't beat around the bush. Mr. Shower Man told the Princess Bride that he would like to spend the entire day getting to know her, and they did just that. They went everywhere from the museum, where they "gazed" at art—more like at each other—to dancing. They spent the entire weekend together and you already know the end of this story. He traveled to France, bringing a beautiful portrait that he had painted of her to express his love. Then she visited him for a month in Germany. Now they want to be together forever, so I guess we really don't know the end of this story.

If you visit the grounds of the Stockholm Royal Palace, you too might fall in love with a European man.

Word to the Wise. The Princess Bride wanted me to pass on to you the technique she developed for shamelessly using see-through showers in hostels. She says the key is to shower when other people aren't around, make it short, and if someone does happen to join you, just act like see-through showering is normal. Then, don't dillydally. Get out fast and meet the European studs when you are wearing something more flattering than soap suds.

Switzerland

Single girls imagining Switzerland visualize majestic snow-covered mountains, skiing down those amazing slopes, and socializing in Alpine towns set off by hills and meadows. Those are exactly the places where my friends have met men, not only from Switzerland, but from all over Europe.

When a Swiss Miss Gave Me the
Lowdown on Swiss Men

A Swiss girlfriend told me with her adorable little accent, "In Switzerland, the guys are a little shyer at first, but once they ask you out they are big on nonverbal approaches for getting to know you." She went on to explain that if an athletic Swiss man wants to take a woman on a date, he will plan something like snowboarding, especially if the woman has never snowboarded. Then he will help her down the slope, knowing that if he lets go of her she might fall. Naturally, chivalry calls for super-close contact in such a situation . . . and if the girl is so bad that she brings down her Swiss man in the process, they have even closer contact. These guys really know how to make the stealth moves for intimacy! They act innocent but my Swiss friend assured me that they are not.

This Swiss girl says that in the broad sense there are two main types of native men: those wanting serious relationships and those wanting "what you call friends with benefits." After making this latter statement, she looked at me with her big blue eyes and exclaimed, "See, I'm getting pretty good at English. I know lots of your sayings, like 'No ring no thing.'" She proceeded to explain that most Swiss men don't generally date a variety of girls at once. They like to "stick to" one girl for a period of time. As for the best places to meet them, she said that the men especially prefer the slopes where they can offer skiing and snowboarding help or the clubs and festivals where they can dance.

My Swiss girlfriend explained that there are also two basic categories of Swiss men who use this latter girl-meeting approach: the guys who are the epitome of Groovers and know how to "do all of the fancy romantic dances like foxtrot," and the ones who "have no steps." Noticing the bewildered look on my face, she elaborated, "They just move to the music and dance really close . . . I mean really, really close." I told her that in English we call that dance the "bump and grind." She replied, "Awesome. Now I have another phrase to add to my English repertoire." The only problem was that she started using these phrases in her English essays. I don't think any professor would appreciate "The History of the Bump and Grind" as a scholarly work. Anyway, this Swiss girl said that no matter whether you are doing the foxtrot or the bump and grind, the goal of every Swiss man is for the two of you to get so hot that he can ask you to join him outside. If you are already outside dancing at a festival, he will want to ask you to walk away from the crowd with him to get some fresh air.

MAN-MEETING TIDBIT. Communicating with Swiss men in their native tongue can be a bit tricky because the country has many different dialects. Depending on the sector, citizens speak German, French, or Italian. In some places they speak a hybrid of languages, like Swiss-German, which is basically German with a Swiss twist. Don't worry! Your pantomiming skills will work in all of these modes.

Now that you're in on the Swiss men, it's time to discover the road-tested hot spots where you can meet them.

Bernese Oberland (Lauterbrunnen Valley)

Lauterbrunnen Valley, located a little south of Interlaken, is home to about seventy-two stunning waterfalls that seem to have minds of their own as they go crashing over the rocks. Staubbach, the highest waterfall in Switzerland, drops six hundred feet and cascades around the valley's entrance. Depending on the weather conditions and time of year, this breathtaking view attracts many mountain bikers, hikers, skiers, snowboarders, and BASE jumpers—who are total risk revelers. They jump off of cliffs generally at low altitudes with little time to deploy their parachutes and basically no time to deal with upcoming problems. Most BASE jumpers here are males who just cross their fingers, hope for the best, and want to meet the single girls after landing.

The strong effects of Mother Nature in Lauterbrunnen can be quite spontaneous and avalanches are common, so I'd suggest hiring a guide. Then not only will you meet European men, you will stay safe. None of my friends who have visited this valley used guides, but they were very familiar with the area and were practically professional athletes seasoned at dealing with nature's unexpected twists.

Lauterbrunnen's lively waterfalls do not destroy the tranquility of this town, and everything I read about it says the nightlife is a snoozer, but that is *not* what my girlfriends who have visited report. This beautiful valley has an undercover party scene. The key to enjoying it is to get in tight with locals.

When Athena Was Escorted to the Underground Party Scene

A friend of mine who visited is an avid outdoor sports chick. Let's call her Athena, after the Greek goddess known for being athletic and resilient. Many of Athena's friends are strong guys, so naturally many of her travel buddies are also guys. She could always keep up with them, but unfortunately whenever they biked, hiked, or climbed together in Europe, the local men assumed that she was in a relationship. She said that she should have made matching shirts for her group reading, "Just because we're together, doesn't mean we're dating."

Athena traveled to Lauterbrunnen with a close guy friend who I like to call Tyr, after the Norse sports god. After a few exciting days of biking and hiking in the valley and a few chill nights of hanging out in one of the town's few pubs until 11 PM when the sidewalks rolled up, Athena wanted some European man adventures—preferably ones that didn't die off before midnight. Since everyone in the area thought that she and Tyr were a couple, Athena asked Tyr if he would help her set them straight. She had her eye on two sexy Swedish BASE jumping guides, so she persuaded Tyr to meet them, clue them in on their relationship, get the scoop on their love lives, and score an invite to hang out together with them at the pub that evening. Athena didn't know that she was going to be in for so much more than just hanging out with these hotties.

When Tyr returned from his mission, he reported that the guides had been visiting Lauterbrunnen for several years in between work as body doubles in films where they did the kind of ridiculous stunts that make you gasp. They had come to the valley so much that they were considered locals. They wanted Athena and Tyr to join them for drinks at the pub that evening.

After the sun set Athena had two magnificent European options sitting at her table. When the bartender called for last drinks at eleven she thought she might have to turn in early again. Instead the guides whispered to her and Tyr, "When everyone leaves, quietly follow us." After the tabs were closed and the travelers cleared out, the guides led Athena and Tyr through the back door, around the building, in a side door, and up the stairs, where an intimate dance party of about fifteen Europeans was in full swing with a sports hunk playing DJ and spinning hits. The guides explained that the pub owners turned the second floor into a secret club on many nights after the business shut down. Athena reported that as the night went on, the party grew more vivacious and larger, but the feel of this bash never departed from the feel of the Lauterbrunnen Valley—intimate and small, the perfect scenario for striking up a relationship with a Laut lover.

Athena now works in Europe and is still close to some of the European men that she met on her first night of partying in Lauterbrunnen.

Word to the Wise. The Lauterbrunnen Valley is known to have several of these types of parties, but trying to sneak in is not a smart tactic. That won't leave a good impression on your European prospects. So follow Athena's example and get to know some locals during the day. Then join them for drinks and let them escort you into the secret clubs. Also, if you are traveling with a guy, let the European men know that you are single. You could always try Athena's shirt idea. Actually, she now has a European boyfriend, so custom shirts are no longer necessary.

Pays-d'Enhaut
(Château-d'Oex International Balloon Festival)

Pays-d'Enhaut is a district in the canton of Vaud, which is anchored by the town of Château-d'Oex, with a beautiful castle on a hill overlooking the stunning countryside. This enchanting haunt is not normally considered a man-meeting gem, but the International Balloon Festival brings out the Swiss men.

Typically, during the last week in January, Château-d'Oex is buzzing in a blaze of color. An eclectic assortment of more than 130 balloons from twenty different countries is set free in this quaint little village. The balloons rise in unison through the mountains and disappear into the sky.

You can settle in for an entire week of excitement. Enjoy the freedom of flight by trying a variety of sports from paragliding to parachute drops. But remember, the absolute no-miss of this festival is the traditional Night Glow, when a company of balloons performs a nocturnal ballet followed by an extravagant display of fireworks. Don't think this event just attracts gaggles of girls. European men come to see the spectacle and the girls, who they know go for this sort of deal. The best view is from the top of Church Hill. If you can seduce that special Swiss into hanging around after the show, Church Hill might as well be renamed Love Hill. Gazing at the stars is the perfect romantic postlude.

If you don't get that lucky, hope is just down the hill. Throughout the town, the party lives on—with street artists, bonfires, and sensitive hunks. Toss that hair and turn on the charm! Charisma is the key to meeting the man you seek.

Word to the Wise. For the Château-d'Oex International Balloon Festival schedule of events go to www.ballonchateaudoex.ch/sibac. asp?Lang=EN.

If you plan a trip around this winter event you can not only experience it but also the neighboring **Gstaad Valley**, rumored to have the world's most beautiful mountain resort. **Gstaad's "Super Ski Region"** encompasses ten interconnected villages and attracts famous celebrities. It has skiing and snowboarding possibilities for all levels of expertise from beginners to the advanced. Nearby **Diablerets Glacier** is open winter and summer. For you adrenaline aficionados, it even offers heli-skiing. So no matter what your level of skiing expertise, you can enjoy letting the Swiss men "help" you down the slopes.

Château-d'Oex is only about an hour and a half by car from **Geneva**, Switzerland's skiing and snowboarding center, and Geneva is fairly close to other European man-meeting hot spots. The thrill-provoking slopes of **Verbier** are about one hour and forty minutes away, France's **Chamonix** ski terrain is about two hours away, and **Lauterbrunnen** is roughly three hours away. As for Geneva's nightlife, **Lausanne**, located at the shores of Lake Geneva, prides itself on its trendy, man-attracting clubs. With all of this excitement not far from Château-d'Oex, you won't want to miss the International Balloon Festival before or after hitting the slopes and taking in the nightlife.

Verbier (The Slopes)

Verbier, a village in the southwestern canton of Valais, is the daredevil's winter skiing and snowboarding delight—steep, scary, and dangerously difficult. Do you like to live on the edge? Do you thrive off of white-knuckle skiing? Are you so athletic that you can out-bench-press most men? If so, you're in for a treat. The exhilarating routes of sunny Verbier run so high that you can even admire Mont Blanc in France while you are admiring the Swiss men. Verbier's slopes are the center for crazy skiing and snowboarding excitement, the kind you can only find when your adrenaline is pumping so fast that the definition of the word reckless is erased from your mind. The appetite-whetting European men come here to push the envelope, so this hot spot is the hottest for girlies who can keep up with these buff beaus.

If you're a gal who can only handle the bunny hill at best and are with a group of ladies who want to live large at Verbier, you can still meet the guys. You just have to go a different route. I advise spending some time on the easy ski routes to get the experience and then exploring the many other options this hub has to offer. Go to the ice rink or the tennis courts, stroll down the street for some window-shopping, and splash on over to the sports center, with its spacious swimming pool where the guys are said to wind down after an intense day on the slopes. And of course you don't have to be an expert skiing studette to join in on the nightlife, which Verbier is also famous for. Girls have reported meeting European men at the restaurants, bars, and clubs around town.

So don't feel bad if you're not up—or maybe I should say down—for the gigantic vertical drops. You can still stay in the thick of things and tantalize the men.

 MAN-MEETING TIDBIT. Verbier attracts buff European gents with stamina and drive. These are the ideal qualifications not only for conquering Verbier's heart-pounding routes but also for creating unforgettable dates afterward. It will allow them to spend all day schussing down the slopes and remain fresh to party the night away with you.

Verbier (Verbier Ride)

For chicks who thrive on competition, the Verbier Ride is a rare opportunity. It began in 1999 as an event for accomplished skiers that was fun, friendly, and filled with camaraderie, while remaining extremely challenging. In no time, it morphed into an important competition with sponsored rides and professional athletes. Although the event is now prestigious, it has in no way adopted a snooty attitude. Amity is still the glue that holds this sporting affair together.

The Verbier Ride is open to any capable skier. And by "capable" I mean capable of participating in one of the most difficult competitions in the world. If you want to do this, I have three words of advice for you—train, train, and train. When you've done that, train some more.

♥ MAN-MEETING TIDBIT. The promoters of the Verbier Ride want to give professional-skier wannabes and soon-to-be's the chance to challenge the skiing stars. In other words, to them this event is "competing with the skiing stars." Since it is based on friendly bonding, you could consider it more like "dating the skiing stars." What could you be in for? Oh, only having drinks at an after-party with some of the most popular skiers that you see on the news winning elite medals. No big deal right? *Wrong!*

Word to the Wise. Check out www.verbierride.com to view the events taking place at the next Verbier Ride.

Multi-Country
Man-Meeting
Sports Events

Any Country (Any Sport)

Every European country has various professional sporting events ranging from rodeos to car races. You really can't go wrong by attending these shindigs, because men dig them.

Soccer is especially popular with European men. At every game I attended, at least 90 percent of the bleachers were taken over by testosterone. I greatly admire the athleticism of these types of players, but I had never really gotten into the sport before coming to Europe. So I was very surprised to find that I couldn't get enough of European soccer, and it wasn't just the action on the field that kept me coming back for more. I will admit that it didn't matter to my girlfriends and me what team racked up the most points. The real winner was always the team that had the most players with the best butts. And wow, European soccer players are definitely in the wrong field. They should really be men's underwear and jeans models.

Anyway, back to meeting European men. The locals come alive at sporting events. It's hard to even think over their boisterous shouting and chanting, and it's really best to join in. If you rise to your feet, raise your hands in the air, and join in on their chants—which are always easy to pick up even if they are in a foreign language—the males will notice you and plan an introduction when the game ends.

Meeting Men After Soccer Games. After the clock runs out, it is imperative that you refrain from jumping on the first subway and heading back to your hotel. Like at the Festival of San Juan, it will be so packed that you will get smushed.

Plus, if you leave right away, you're going to miss out on the bar scene. Most soccer fields and other popular sports venues are surrounded by pubs. Guys typically stick around and party after the final point is scored. No matter what the outcome, drinks are typically on the men. Whether they are toasting out of celebration or drowning their sorrows from a loss, they will want the company of you girls . . . especially if you show enthusiasm for their team. It doesn't matter if you don't know diddly-squat about the sport, they will happily explain every minutia. And if you are a sports connoisseur, that's even better. They will revel in the fact that you can hold your own in a discussion dissecting the game.

The best part of these post-game activities is that the players often make appearances at these bars after showering off. So, if you find your way there, you may just get to enjoy the back shanks view up close and personal. One of my friends even went out with a player from a "winning" European team!

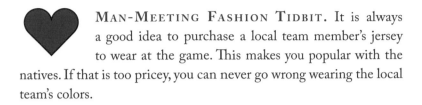

MAN-MEETING FASHION TIDBIT. It is always a good idea to purchase a local team member's jersey to wear at the game. This makes you popular with the natives. If that is too pricey, you can never go wrong wearing the local team's colors.

Word to the Wise. All professional sporting events are in very high demand. Make sure to buy your tickets way in advance or they will probably be sold out. Also, make sure to buy them in the section of the stadium for the home country's team. This may sound kind of ridiculous, but I have made the mistake of sitting in the wrong section, and it didn't score me any points with the locals. The experience was especially uncomfortable since I was being very supportive by wearing the home team's jersey. Worst of all, the home team lost! I was able to redeem myself in the sports bar afterward, but don't make my mistake. Double-check the seating diagrams. They can be confusing, especially when you are in countries with language barriers.

France, Italy, and Switzerland (Tour de Mont Blanc)

Tour de Mont Blanc is a hut-to-hut hiking trip through France, Italy, and Switzerland that Europeans rave about. Typically it takes about ten days, but those with legs of lighting can make it through in a substantially shorter amount of time. Keep in mind, though, that if you want to meet the local men, going ultra-fast will not win that race.

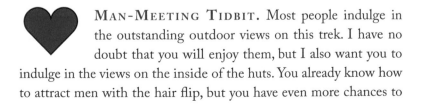

MAN-MEETING TIDBIT. Most people indulge in the outstanding outdoor views on this trek. I have no doubt that you will enjoy them, but I also want you to indulge in the views on the inside of the huts. You already know how to attract men with the hair flip, but you have even more chances to get to know the hiking guys in the huts. Ten days of touring means ten nights of happy hutting and deciding which natives you would like to lead you on the rest of the journey.

Each hut generally holds about one hundred inhabitants who are forced to get quite comfortable with each other quite fast. Cots are placed side by side, mixing genders. Bathroom facilities are not segregated for men and women, so you will know everyone intimately within no time. This means that you better look awfully cute in your PJs.

Word to the Packing Wise. Don't be targeted as the typical tourist who brings her entire life in a gigantic backpack. There is no need to lug a trillion pounds down the road. By the second day, you would be so sore that you couldn't enjoy the experience. Your highly toned European trailblazer may offer to take over the load, but you will most likely wear out your welcome before he has reached the peak in your relationship. A day pack is more than sufficient—along with a thin towel that will dry overnight and travel sizes of soap, shampoo, conditioner, a toothbrush, toothpaste, deodorant, hair bands, PJs, minimal changes of clothes, and a thin sleeping bag liner for the cots. The huts are convenient and provide food, beverages, and all other facilities that you will need during the night. They make it easy to travel so you can just enjoy the journey.

Hiking Routes. There are several routes you can take in Tour de Mont Blanc. Many books and websites provide details, but I recommend *The Tour of Mont Blanc: Complete Two-Way Trekking Guide* by Kev Reynolds. This book provides detailed instructions and maps for various tours as well as the names and numbers of huts along each route. It is wise to call in advance and secure reservations.

Final Word to the Wise. I have heard that the best time weather-wise for hiking is between May and September.

Au Revoir

Friends have told me that I should have majored in European Party Studies with a minor in Clubology. Sadly, Vanderbilt University had no such curriculum, so I wrote my own syllabus. I hope this book enriches your European adventures and helps you ignite European relationships!

Besos,
Katherine Chloé Cahoon

Telephone Tips

Phoning can be quite tricky in the EU with the variety of European country codes and procedures. I think this is why Skype is so popular there. This mode of communication is also a great option to use with your European men because you can see them while you talk. If they are Airbrushed, that's all the more reason to log on to Skype! Still, having a phone in Europe is imperative because it is portable. You can always have it on hand, and it will help keep you safe.

Getting an International Phone

There are a variety of ways to go about getting a foreign phone. I rented one in the States and took it with me. That way, I had it the instant I landed in the European airport. It really came in handy. Before I left on one trip, my Spanish *señora* asked me to call her the second I arrived in Madrid so she could be waiting for me outside her home. Luckily, I already had my international phone packed.

Many companies rent out international phones. I used PicCell Wireless on my last trip (https://www.piccellwireless.com). The company was extremely reliable and the employees were helpful. If you want to search around for the company with the best price, Google "International Cell Phone Rentals." Prices can vary, so I'd advise rechecking each time you visit Europe. If you have an unlocked GSM phone, then you can just rent a SIM card from any of the cell phone rentals.

Another option is to get a cell phone in Europe. Every country deals with this differently, so feasibility is dependent on where you are staying. When I studied in London, a number of the students waited until they arrived to find a phone because there was an international phone store just up the street from our dorms.

If you already have a cell with a built in "world phone capability," then it is designed to work in Europe, but according to Verizon, the international connection can be spotty.

Making Calls in Europe

In the UK, the calling instructions from country to country are so varied that many of my girlfriends with international phones curtailed their calls to save their sanity. I don't want that to happen to you. If you want to make a call to any country, I want you to be able to do it with ease, so I'm giving you a telephone chart and dialing instructions to take along. In my opinion, it is impossible to improve upon Rick Steves' approach. He knows how to make international calls like you girls now know how to meet European men, and he was kind enough to help. He doesn't want you to have any problems returning calls to your hot European honeys. Here is his foreign phoning 411.

Making Calls Within European Countries

About half of all European countries use area codes (like the US)— the other half uses a direct-dial system without area codes.

To make calls within a country that uses a direct-dial system (Belgium, the Czech Republic, Denmark, France, Greece, Italy, Norway, Poland, Portugal, Spain, and Switzerland), you dial the same number whether you're calling across the country or across the street.

In countries that use area codes (such as Austria, Croatia, Britain, Finland, Germany, Hungary, Ireland, the Netherlands, Slovakia, Slovenia, Sweden, and Turkey), you dial the local number when calling within a city, and you add the area code if calling long distance within the country. Example: to call a Munich hotel (089-264-349) from within Munich, dial 264-349; to call it from Frankfurt, dial 089-264-349.

Note that some countries, particularly those with area codes, can have phone numbers of varying lengths. For instance, a hotel might have a seven-digit phone number and an eight-digit fax number.

Making International Calls

Always start with the international access code (011 if you're calling from America or Canada, 00 from anywhere in Europe). If you see a phone number that begins with +, you have to replace the + with the international access code. Then dial the country code of the country you're calling (see chart on pages 252–253).

What you dial next depends on the phone system of the country you're calling. If the country uses area codes, drop the initial zero of the area code, then dial the rest of the number. Example: to call the Munich hotel (089-264-349) from Italy, dial 00, then 49 (Germany's country code), then 89-264-349.

Countries that use direct-dial systems vary in how they're accessed internationally by phone. For instance, if you're making an international call to Denmark, the Czech Republic, Italy, Norway, Portugal, or Spain, simply dial the international access code, country code, and phone number. Example: to call a Madrid hotel (915-212-900) from Germany, dial 00, 34 (Spain's country code), then 915-212-900. But if you're calling Belgium, France, Poland, or Switzerland, drop the initial zero of the phone number. Example: to call a Paris hotel (01-47-05-49-15) from London, dial 00, then 33 (France's country code), then 1-47-05-49-15 (the phone number without an initial zero).

Calling Home

Remember, from most of Europe, it's six hours earlier in New York and nine hours earlier in California. To dial direct, first enter the international access code (00 from Europe), then the country code of the US (1), then the area code and the seven-digit number.

European Calling Chart

AC = Area Code; LN = Local Number

Country	Country Code	Calling within	Calling from the US/Canada	Calling from another European country
Austria	43	AC + LN	011 + 43 + AC (without initial zero) + LN	00 + 43 + AC (without initial zero) + LN
Belgium	32	LN	011 + 32 + LN (without initial zero)	00 + 32 + LN (without initial zero)
Bosnia-Herzegovina	387	AC + LN	011 + 387 + AC (without initial zero) + LN	00 + 387 + AC (without initial zero) + LN
Britain	44	AC + LN	011 + 44 + AC (without initial zero) + LN	00 + 44 + AC (without initial zero) + LN
Croatia	385	AC + LN	011 + 385 + AC (without initial zero) + LN	00 + 385 + AC (without initial zero) + LN
Czech Republic	420	AC + LN	011 + 420 + LN	00 + 420 + LN

Country	Country Code	Calling within	Calling from the US/Canada	Calling from another European country
Denmark	45	LN	011 + 45 + LN	00 + 45 + LN
Estonia	372	LN	011 + 372 + LN	00 + 372 + LN
Finland	358	AC + LN	011 + 358 + AC (without initial zero) + LN	999 + 358 + AC (without initial zero) + LN
France	33	LN	011 + 33 + LN (without initial zero)	00 + 33 + LN (without initial zero)
Germany	49	AC + LN	011 + 49 + AC (without initial zero) + LN	00 + 49 + AC (without initial zero) + LN
Greece	30	LN	011 + 30 + LN	00 + 30 + LN
Hungary	36	06 + AC + LN	011 + 36 + AC + LN	00 + 36 + AC + LN
Ireland	353	AC + LN	011 + 353 + AC (without initial zero) + LN	00 + 353 + AC (without initial zero) + LN
Italy	39	LN	011 + 39 + LN	00 + 39 + LN
Montenegro	382	AC + LN	011 + 382 + AC (without initial zero) + LN	00 + 382 + AC (without initial zero) + LN
Netherlands	31	AC + LN	011 + 31 + AC (without initial zero) + LN	00 + 31 + AC (without initial zero) + LN
Norway	47	LN	011 + 47 + LN	00 + 47 + LN
Poland	48	LN	011 + 48 + LN (without initial zero)	00 + 48 + LN (without initial zero)
Portugal	351	LN	011 + 351 + LN	00 + 351 + LN
Slovakia	421	AC + LN	011 + 421 + AC (without initial zero) + LN	00 + 421 + AC (without initial zero) + LN
Slovenia	386	AC + LN	011 + 386 + AC (without initial zero) + LN	00 + 386 + AC (without initial zero) + LN
Spain	34	LN	011 + 34 + LN	00 + 34 + LN
Sweden	46	AC + LN	011 + 46 + AC (without initial zero) + LN	00 + 46 + AC (without initial zero) + LN
Switzerland	41	LN	011 + 41 + LN (without initial zero)	00 + 41 + LN (without initial zero)
Turkey	90	AC (if no initial zero is included, add one) + LN	011 + 90 + AC (without initial zero) + LN	00 + 90 + AC (without initial zero) + LN

- The preceding instructions apply whether you're calling a landline or a mobile phone.

- The international access codes (the first numbers you dial when making an international call) are 011 if you're calling from the USA/Canada, or 00 if you're calling from virtually anywhere in Europe (except Finland, where it's 999).

- To call the US or Canada from Europe, dial 00, then 1 (the country code for the US and Canada), then the area code and number. In short, 00+1+AC+LN.

Excerpted from *Europe Through the Back Door* with permission from Rick Steves. To learn more about Rick Steves and European travel, visit ricksteves.com.

Single Girl's
Slangtionary

About Business: European men who are successful entrepreneurs, doctors, engineers, writers, advertising execs, bankers, photographers, or consultants. See page 107.

Airbrushed: European men who have absolutely flawless features with seemingly no effort. See page 108.

Amante: Spanish word meaning "lover."

Ambitieux: French word meaning "ambitious"; often describes go-get-'em guys.

Artsy: European men who know everything about art and will tell you romantic love stories. See page 109.

¡Ay caramba!: Spanish phrase that is the equivalent of "Oh my!"

Bird: British slang for an attractive female.

Bloke: British slang for "man."

Bonito: Spanish word meaning "pretty."

Butterfly: Describes a girl who is a social butterfly.

Caballeros: Spanish word meaning "gentlemen."

CDs: Committal Daters—girls who like having boyfriends. They enjoy being in serious relationships. See page 7.

Charismats: European men who are naturally suave and witty without appearing to put on a show or trying too hard to impress you. See page 109.

Charmant: French word meaning "charming."

Churros con chocolate: Spanish desert that is eaten after dipping pastry into a very rich, thick hot chocolate.

CYA: Cover Your Ass.

Date Card: Lined index card with each line marked as a different day of the week. It is a convenient way to keep your dates straight, which is not so easy to do in foreign countries with language barriers. Tuck it in your cute clutch.

DO-YA: Dropped On Your Ass—pronounced "Do ya?" As in, "Do ya wanna be dropped on your ass?" I don't think so! A girl gets the DO-YA from a guy when he dumps her abruptly.

Dub: An Irish guy from Dublin.

El guapo: Spanish phrase meaning "the handsome one."

EMCT: European Male Commitment Test, as follows. See answer analysis on page 98.

1. When you are alone with your European man, does he:

A. Express the desire to date you and only you, and then ask how you feel about him? Is all of this done on his own initiative, without any coaxing on your part?

B. Express the desire to date you and only you, and then tell you what a nice ass you have?

C. Never bring up the desire to date you and only you?

2. When you ask to meet his friends, does he:

A. Make up excuses for why you can't?

B. Proudly introduce you to many of his friends?

C. Only introduce you to a handful of his friends?

3. When you ask about his family, does he:

A. Skirt the issue?

B. Say very little?

C. Invite you to meet them? Or, if they do not live nearby, tell you as much as you want to know about them?

Extremamente ridículo: Spanish phrase meaning "extremely ridiculous."

Férfi: Hungarian word meaning "man."

Fiesta-ed: Spanglish for "partied." Similarly, "fiesta-ing" is Spanglish for "partying."

Followers: Girls who want to meet the men, but never do. They travel in packs, generally going to Europe with large groups of friends and never breaking away from them the whole time. See page 8.

Fun Seekers: Girls who are out to make fun all the time. See page 9.

Gafas: European men who are fun and goofy. Having them around is always a delight. See page 110.

Gift Grabbers: Girls who want to be given gifts without giving anything in return. See page 10.

GLAD: Girls Love Adventure Day.

GRGG: Getting Rescued by a Gorgeous Guy—pronounced like the guy's name Gregg.

Groovers: Groovy European guys who are phenomenal dancers. See page 110.

Hei: Finnish word meaning "hello."

Ho-dough: Money earned by a hooker.

Hombre de negocios: Spanish phrase meaning "businessman."

Hombres: Spanish word meaning "men."

Homme à femmes: French for a Don Juan or Romeo.

Hommes: French word meaning "men."

Hot cat: Hottie.

How bad!: An Irish phrase meaning "good."

Jack: A sweet and sensitive hunk; named in honor of Jack Dawson from the movie *Titanic*.

Kissers: Girls who plan to kiss a guy from every European country they visit. See page 10.

Kuop: A Finnish guy from Kuopio.

Landy: A guy from the Netherlands.

Manmarks: Man landmarks.

Man-Meeting Dance Floor Formula:

> Step 1: As you enter the dance floor scan the room for male potential.
>
> Step 2: Strategically place yourself near your target.
>
> Step 3: Keep glancing at him until he looks at you.
>
> Step 4: Encouragingly smile.
>
> Step 5: Look away and dance one of your best moves. See Tip #30 on page 82.

Männer: German word meaning "men."

Manopolize: To be monopolized by men.

Mantastic: Full of fantastic men.

Mint: Attractive man who is especially talented in his kissing technique.

Moochers: The one type of European guy to stay away from. Moochers are unemployed and live with their parents way into adulthood if not forever. See page 111.

MOS: Member of the Opposite Sex.

NCDs: Non-Committal Daters—girls who want to go on several dates with different types of European men but are not in the committing mood. See page 11.

Noche: Spanish word meaning "night."

Outdoor Sports Aficionados: These outdoor European hunks have the most enviable bodies, generally laid-back personalities, and intense athletic motivation. See page 112.

Paraíso: Spanish word meaning "paradise."

PDA: Public Display of Affection

Princess Brides: Girls who are looking for the Mr. European Love of Their Lives. See page 12.

REI: Recreational Equipment Inc. This is a corporation that sells sporting and outdoor recreation apparel and equipment.

Rock Stars: There are two types in this European male category, Collegiate and Not-So-Collegiate. See page 112.

SAD: Singles' Awareness Day.

SAM: Sought After Man—pronounced like the guy's name. This term can be used to stealthily inform a girlfriend of a nearby hot European male. For example, "SAM is standing behind you" or, "SAM sighting by the bar."

Samplers: Girls who are only in Europe for a short stay and who try to sample as much of Europe as they can. See page 12.

Sexcapaders: Girls who want to get laid in every European country they visit. See page 12.

SGA: Single Girls' Association.

Slightly Sleazy: These European men are often entertaining, nice guys, but they put a new definition on the phrase "lovin' the single girls." They will want to be all over you. See page 113.

Social Chairs: Girls who are the leaders of the followers. See page 13.

SURF: A way to meet male surfers or kiteboarders, as described by one of them. The acronym stands for: **S**unscreen; **U**naware that you are trying to attract guys; **R**ide: get on the board and try it; and **F**ind a cute surfing or boarding instructor and sign up for lessons. See pages 169–171.

Taly: A guy from Italy.

TDH: Tall, Dark, and Handsome.

Wower: A male that is so wonderful all you can say is "wow!"

European Hot Spot Index

(There are bustling bars in many of the nice neighborhoods of major cities. See each country for details.)